Living In Hope

*Cycle C Sermons
Based on the Second Lessons for Lent and Easter*

Bonnie Bates

CSS Publishing Company, Inc

Lima, Ohio

LIVING IN HOPE

FIRST EDITION
Copyright © 2021
by CSS Publishing Co., Inc.

The original purchaser may print and photocopy material in this publication for use as it was intended (worship material for worship use; educational material for classroom use; dramatic material for staging or production). No additional permission is required from the publisher for such copying by the original purchaser only. Inquiries should be addressed to: Permissions, CSS Publishing Company, Inc., 5450 N. Dixie Highway, Lima, Ohio 45807.

Library of Congress Cataloging-in-Publication Data:

Names: Bates, Bonnie, author. Title: Living in hope : Cycle C sermons based on second lesson for Lent and Easter / Bonnie Bates. Description: First edition. | Lima, Ohio : CSS Publishing Company, Inc., [2021] Identifiers: LCCN 2021002024 | ISBN 9780788030246 (paperback) | ISBN 9780788030253 (ebook) Subjects: LCSH: Bible. Gospels--Sermons. | Common lectionary (1992). Year C. | Lenten sermons. | Easter--Sermons. | Church year sermons. Classification: LCC BV4277 .B34 2021 | DDC 252/.62--dc23 LC record available at https://lccn.loc.gov/2021002024

For more information about CSS Publishing Company resources, visit our website at www.csspub.com, email us at csr@csspub.com, or call (800) 241-4056.

e-book:
ISBN-13: 978-0-7880-3025-3
ISBN-10: 0-7880-3025-6

ISBN-13: 978-0-7880-3024-6
ISBN-10: 0-7880-3024-8   DIGITALLY PRINTED

This book is dedicated to all the saints of the church, past, present, and future. May we all continue to live in the hope of God's presence and love.

Content

Living Through Hard Times   7
Ash Wednesday
2 Corinthians 5:20b-6:10

Faithfulness in These Days   12
First Sunday in Lent
Romans 10:8b-13

Standing Firm   17
Second Sunday in Lent
Philippians 3:17-4:1

Seeking the Presence of God   22
Third Sunday in Lent
1 Corinthians 10:1-13

A New Creation in Hope   27
Fourth Sunday in Lent
2 Corinthians 5:16-21

Pressing on in Faith   31
Fifth Sunday in Lent
Philippians 3:4b-14

Love Lives   36
Liturgy of the Passion / Sixth Sunday in Lent
Philippians 2:5-11

At the Table   42
Maundy Thursday
1 Corinthians 11:23-26

We Build the Tomb   47
Good Friday
Hebrews 10:16-25

We Live in Hope   52
Resurrection of the Lord
1 Corinthians 15: 19-26

Visions of Hope   57
Second Sunday of Easter
Revelation 1:4-8

My Redeemer Lives   62
Third Sunday of Easter
Revelation 5:11-14

Peace in the Presence   66
Fourth Sunday of Easter
Revelation 7:9-17

Transformed and Transforming   71
Fifth Sunday of Easter
Revelation 21:1-6

The Mountain Top   76
Sixth Sunday of Easter
Revelation 21:10, 22-22:5

The Balcony View   82
Ascension of the Lord
Ephesians 1:15-23

The Beginning and The End   86
Seventh Sunday of Easter
Revelation 22:12-14, 16-17, 20-21

Ash Wednesday

2 Corinthians 5:20b-6:10

Living Through Hard Times

Sometimes it is hard for us to accept the hardships of this life. Certainly, in the current situation, with so many people in so many communities and countries still affected by the COVID-19 pandemic, there is much worry and anxiety. Yet, worry and struggle have been a part of the human condition almost as long as human beings have been on the earth.

As Paul wrote this second letter to the church in Corinth, he was reminding the people that he, too had struggled: "in beatings, imprisonments, and riots; in hard work, sleepless nights and hunger" (2 Corinthians 6:5). His life, as follower of Jesus and as evangelist had been difficult, more difficult in some ways than our Christian lives have been. We, in the United States at least, are rarely beaten or imprisoned for our faith. We may have had hard work to do and some sleepless nights, but most of us have food to eat, homes to rest in, and places to be safe with other believers. What if it were not so?

When I was touring two dioceses of the Church of South India in February 2020, I watched people walk into small concrete buildings and sit on the floor for worship. I spoke with people who had walked for eight to ten kilometers to worship on Sundays or Holy Days. I sat with people at a table who shared the last they had to eat with us American visitors. I was honored and blessed and humbled to be with people of such faith and generosity. Having been a Christian all my life, I have rarely in a US church, save perhaps a Pentecostal church, seen people worshiping with such energy and celebration of the presence of the Holy Spirit. I learned a lot from these people; I have, I hope, brought forth much that I learned into my ministry here in the United States.

Living in Hope

For one thing, I understand suffering and dedication in a different way. I have never had to walk miles to get to church — even when snowstorms blocked the roads, my walk was several blocks, not several miles. I have been at the poverty level, but I have never gone without food for days or had to walk to a community well to access water. While I have been a faithful churchgoer and, I hope, disciple of Jesus, my life has been comparatively simple. I was never beaten or imprisoned or had no place to live and no food to eat. I have been safe in the expressions of my faith and my church participation.

In a primarily Hindu nation, with increasing Muslim faith citizens, India has only 12% of its population following Jesus. Yes, there is great joy, great fervor, and yet a recognition that all the people are children of God. For the most part, unless encouraged by the government to behave in alternative ways, the population is at peace with one another — no matter their faith traditions. I actually preached at a community festival, the Siluvaggutta Jathara at Gangaram, a rural festival attended by Christians, Muslims, Hindis, and those with no faith at all. More than 1,000 people gathered to hear me preach from the gospel of Jesus Christ. There was no heckling, no shaming, no ignoring my message — rather there were tears in the eyes of women, participation and affirmation, clapping and cheering at the conclusion of the message, and a deep sense of reverence in the attention paid to me. I cannot imagine a US group, even of a variety of Christian denominations, being more engaged and more attentive to the words of my mouth, which I know were the words God asked me to share. This reconciling of the people gathered as simply children of God, not of sects or faith traditions, was a profound experience of faith and reconciliation for me.

When Paul wrote of reconciliation, I am not sure this is what he was speaking about. He wanted us to remove the barriers and not be stumbling blocks to people of faith. And yet, Paul commended us to "in every way… in purity, understanding, patience and kindness; in the Holy Spirit and in sincere love; in truthful speech and in the power of God; with weapons of righteousness in the right hand and in the left" to open our hearts to our siblings in Christ. How powerful! How amazing the world might be if we focused on purity, understanding, patience, and kindness — all gifts of the Holy Spirit. What might change in our relationships, in our faith communities, in our families, in our towns, states, and nations, if we focused on righteousness, sincere love, and reconciliation?

As I write this, our nation is still in the throes of a pandemic, still divided over issues of faith, race, and governmental decisions. We still, in the US, focus on our individual perspectives and our individual opinions, sometimes to the detriment of civil conversations and relationships. This seems to me to be the antitheses of the gospel and of Paul's letter to the church in Corinth. We know from studies of this church and through Paul's letters, that there was dissension in this church, arguments as to approach, and some problems with worship (as in the rich waiting until the poor arrived before sharing the community meal). The focus may have been like the attitudes in the US: what I want as an individual is most important and the common good is secondary. Yet, Paul reminded us that the relationships we have with one another are vitally important. Despite suffering and challenges, Paul called us to righteousness, reconciliation, and love.

My second brother died last year. My youngest brother died when he was five and I was twelve, but my remaining brother died last year. He had many challenges and issues in his life, among them addiction to alcohol and drugs. As children we played together, ice skated together, rode bikes together, and played football together in our backyard. We had a competitive but pretty good relationship. As his addictions came into play, we became more and more estranged. He was angrier, I was less tolerant. There were arguments, long periods of silence between us. These were more than sibling rivalry. I began to question if the person he became was actually the brother I knew at all. Some of you may be able to relate to this. The illness of addiction plagues many of us, many families. There is deep pain as relationships are damaged.

I am happy to say that before his death, my brother and I were reconciled. His addictions came to an end, but not before he committed a crime that landed him in prison for the last twelve years of his life. During those twelve years we were able to rebuild our relationship, talk, laugh, write letters, and remember the love we felt for one another. This was truly a gift for me. I know it was for him as well. I thought, after his death, about the wasted years — more than thirty of them — that were lost to us. His creativity, artistic, and carpentry skills were gifts. I have several photographs he took of nature framed and hanging in my home. I think of him often. I could look back with regret, and sometimes I do, but I try to think of our last years together, the years of our reconciliation and renewed relationship, as a gift from God.

The coming together in relationships is what Paul was writing about. Despite any suffering, challenges, pain, and anger we feel, we are called to walk into our relationships with the open heart of love. Paul loved the people of the churches he found, even when they were not behaving in righteous and charitable ways. God loves us even when we are not living and acting in righteous and charitable ways. Please note that Paul wrote of righteousness, not self-righteousness. The righteousness we are called to is the righteousness of God as lived out by Jesus. This righteousness is filled with acts of inclusion, acceptance, love, compassion, and healing. Yes, Jesus reminded us what it means to be siblings who are faithful to God, but rather than judge (except in cases of self-righteousness), Jesus loved. Jesus healed. Jesus wept over the pain people felt and acted to create. Jesus forgave, even from the cross.

Reconciliation is hard. Compassion is sometimes hard. Kindness is sometimes hard. Patience is sometimes hard. Love is sometimes hard. But love is not just what we feel. Love is a commandment, a calling, and a requirement of Jesus' followers. This Lenten season, let us reflect on this all on us as Christians, to love God with our whole selves and to love our neighbor as ourselves. Let us follow the instructions in Paul's letter to build community through the righteousness of God, through our faithfulness, and through our love. Let us be beacons of light and hope in a challenging world, in a challenging time. Pray it will be so. Amen.

First Sunday in Lent

Romans 10:8b-13

Faithfulness In These Days

As we enter the Lenten season, we reflect on the life of Jesus, his ministry, his sacrifice, and his love for us. Paul contrasted, in this letter, the concepts of righteousness to the law and to faith, accenting that righteousness that comes from faith is the more important. The word, God's word, is not distant from us, rather it is near us, near our lips and our heart. Knowing Jesus and proclaiming our faith, these are what brings us into relationship with God.

This passage from Romans reminds us that just as the covenant with the Hebrew people was not remote but engaged within the people, so the covenant through Jesus is engaged with us. We are called to live into the covenant Jesus created for and among us; a renewal of the covenants of old but through his love, ministry, and sacrifice. When we believe in our hearts and say with our mouths that Jesus is Lord, when we proclaim this truth we are justified, we will not be put to shame.

Yet, this is not a license to behave in any way we choose and then profess the words, assuming we will be in relationships with God through Christ. I remember in my youth attending worship and encountering people who seemed very pious on Sunday, but very angry and selfish when I encountered them during the rest of the week. For me, this wasn't a true expression of our relationship with Christ. This wasn't truly professing that Jesus is Lord and living out our faith. The living out of our faith is so important. Yes, our hearts need to be aligned with the will of God. Yes, we are called as Christians to profess the ministry, sacrifice and redemption of Jesus. Yet, we are also called to be living examples of the salvation we know and feel. That salvation

First Sunday in Lent

is open to anyone who professes Jesus.

There are some faith communities that believe a predetermined, preordained number of people can enter into heaven and can be saved for all eternity. The rest of us are just out of luck. Paul's letter seems to decry this notion. Paul repeated, in this letter, the insistence that everyone has access to God in faith. Salvation is not a lottery where some are in and some are out. Rather, salvation is accessible to all who have faith, to all who draw near to God. God draws near to us in prayer, in worship, and in our everyday lives. When we choose to draw near to God, God welcomes us. Salvation is for all the faithful, if our faith is honest and genuine, we are assured of God's grace. When we, any of us, call out to God for help, God is present with is.

Everyone who draws near to God, seeking God's help and hope, is not to be disappointed. Yet, salvation is not so much our seeking, or struggling to be near to Jesus. Rather Christ is drawn near to us through the good news, through the word shared and believed. Although we come together in sanctuaries and churches to seek God, it is affirmed that God is near to us whether we are in a defined sacred place or not. We do not need to be in the "holy" place to encounter Christ. Rather, Christ is where we are.

There is special comfort in knowing that Christ is with us, God is with us wherever we are. Wandering through the world in our everyday lives, we may not always feel Jesus with us — and yet he is there.

I want to recount a story from my own life. In my seminary days, I participated in a spiritual group working through the spiritual exercises of Saint Ignatius. Originally designed as a thirty-day retreat for those determining a call to the religious life, the nineteenth annotation was developed for a weekly experience. Thus, each day of the original program was studied as a week. The first seven weeks were focused on learning about and experiencing the love of God — not superficially, but in our very bones, in the essence of who we were as individuals. Each week we would meet with a spiritual guide and then as a larger group to reflect on our individual study and prayer. The first seven weeks, from my perspective, went really well. Then we moved in the weeks of exploring sin — our own sin. The goal was to see our sin through the eyes of a loving God.

I froze. I didn't want to explore my sin or my sinfulness. I stopped being able to study or even to pray. I managed to get through the first week with some sort of noncommittal comments to my spiritual guide. By the second week, she was on to my avoidance. She asked me what was really going on. I had to admit my fear, my frozenness, and my unwillingness to move forward.

When we came into the large group setting, she had me share my experience. Then she asked me to think of the darkest, dankest place I could. For me that was a basement, with unfinished walls and a dirt floor. It would be very dimly lit but for one ceiling lightbulb. Seepage of water had created pools and muck. The smell was musty and moldy. There were spiders and spiderwebs. The rickety wooden stairs were uncomfortable and there was only one railing. Then she asked the other participants to gather around me and lay hands on me while I closed my eyes and took a deep breath as I pictured myself walking down into the basement of my sinfulness.

I wasn't sure what would happen. I opened the door, in my mind's eye, and the dankness hit me. I paused. I froze for a moment. Then, feeling that I wasn't alone, feeling the hands resting on me, I took a first tentative step. Slowly I stepped onto the next step and then the third and fourth. I, in my mind and heart, was really reluctant to take each step but I continued to gain comfort from the hands lightly laid on me. I kept going — the fifth step.

In the distance across the basement, a light started to shine. As I stood on the stairs, not moving, the light grew brighter and brighter, and I could see a figure in the light. Heaving, taking a deep breath, I tentatively took one more step. As I did, a figure seemed to come out of the light. I couldn't make out features but somehow, I knew it was Jesus. I felt a warmth enter my heart. I breathed a little easier. Yet, I still could not move on the stairs. Surely, I was not worthy enough for my Savior, the Christ, to

First Sunday in Lent

come to me.

Then as the figure became clearer, I saw arms outstretched to me. I stood frozen on the steps, still unable to move. This could not be a welcome for me. Then I heard a soft voice say to me, "Come my child. Come." My fears evaporated. Ignoring my fear, the darkness of the basement of my sin, the dankness I had felt only a moment ago, I raced down the stairs into the embrace of my Savior. I stayed in that embrace for some moments — I have no idea how long. When I reopened my eyes and came back to the room, my own arms were wrapped around me. My friends' hands were still laid on me and tears were running down my cheeks. I was loved. No matter my sinfulness, I was loved.

This was the most profound spiritual experience of my life. I was shown through meditation and prayer that God through Jesus calls me to come, even in my sinfulness. God loves me so very much that I am welcomed, embraced, and reconciled — I am loved, no matter my sinfulness. I knew what it was like to have my sin forgiven, to see my sin through the eyes of God — to see my sin as something that kept me away from God but did not keep God away from me. The distance and separation had been mine.

This forgiveness, welcome, reconciliation, embrace, and love is open to each and every one of us, each person who proclaims their faithfulness to God.

Our forgiveness is not dependent on who we are, where we are, or which church community we worship. Our forgiveness and salvation is a result of our coming into the presence of God, proclaiming our faithfulness, and then being willing to accept the grace offered. In my experience, I had been unwilling to see myself as so beloved of God that nothing I had ever done could keep me from God's love. I know that I truly am beloved of God. God reaches out for us; he calls out for us. Our reconciliation with God, our salvation, is about our turning toward the love of God. Certainly, we need to be sorry for our sins, we need to seek to align our lives more with the God's call on it, but *we are forgiven*. We truly are.

Living in Hope

From Paul we learn that our faithfulness is what keeps us in relationship with God, Jesus, and the Holy Spirit. It is not our denomination, or self-righteousness, that bring us in relationship with God. Rather it is God's promise to be with us always. God extends himself to us. We are blessed in this way. Our task is to speak the words of our faith, to believe in the salvation of the resurrection and then know that our reconciliation, our own resurrection, is promised to us.

I have never encountered the figure of Jesus in prayer or meditation since that day so long ago, but I now have little trouble bringing my sins before the Lord. I know God hears my plea for forgiveness and for strength to walk in my faith. I know I am redeemed. I know I am promised the presence and love of God each and every day of my life. This is the gift of my faith; the gift of that experience long ago which still lives in my heart. This is the gift we can all be assured we will receive. That is God's promise and God's promises are true. I know that to be true. May it also be so for you. Amen.

Second Sunday in Lent

Philippians 3:17-4:1

Standing Firm

The call of Paul in this letter is to stand firm in the Lord, to not falter, to not align our minds on our earthly life but focus on the eternal life to come. Sounds like a big task, doesn't it?

I woke up hearing the words sung by Sidewalk Prophets, but I was remembering the first words of the refrain as "stand firm in the Lord." You should look up the beautiful lyrics online. As I had been thinking about the title I had given for this message, I wondered about the emotions Paul was feeling in this letter to the church at Philippi.

Paul is calling the people to focus on what is promised, rather than what is — the current trials and benefits of this human life. Paul is calling us to know that our home is not here in this place. We are called not to live the letter of the law, not the human interpretation of the word, but to live in the spirit.

Standing firm in the Lord is difficult. It was difficult for Jesus and it is even more difficult for us. Responding to the call of God on our lives isn't always easy. It upsets our plans and changes everything.

I argued with God about my call to the ministry for more than five years. I had completed a BA and a MA degree in organization and human resource development. I was respected in my workplace and in my field. I was seen as a skilled leader and even began teaching. I was teaching at the college from which I received my MA degree. I was active in church life and firm in my faith. Yet, I couldn't see myself as giving all that up, as shifting my focus from the work I loved and was good at to the call God had placed on my heart. Every time I felt this call, I would volunteer to do another job at the church: serving on the program and outreach committee, teaching Sunday school and confirmation, serving on the governing board, first as vice-chair and then as chair. I just kept sidestepping that call. Arguing with God that he must be making a mistake in calling me. I was in my forties, a woman separated from her husband; I was a mother and grandmother. Answering a call to the ministry just wasn't possible.

Yet, God holds us firmly, challenges us to be who we are called to be, and then ensures we are equipped to perform the tasks, the ministry laid before us. I attended a workshop on a Saturday with my pastor. The focus was engaging youth in worship — funny how after more than twenty years I remember this so clearly. As I was driving us back to the parsonage, I, still feeling this distinct call, asked my pastor about the Lay Education Program. You see, I had another compromise for God. I would become a lay minister, able to lead worship but not becoming an ordained pastor — although that was where God was calling me to journey.

As I pulled into the drive, my pastor laid his hand on my shoulder and asked the question, "Why are you limiting yourself to the Lay Leadership program?" That question opened the floodgates. I was able to share my battle with this call. I was able to explain my fear — going back to school, becoming a pastor, what if I did it badly? What if I wasn't capable? What if, as a pastor, I hurt someone? Besides, I had a job, a house, a life! Did God really want me to change all that? We talked for more than two hours. My pastor sent me home to pray and continue to discern.

As I arrived home, I realized I was simply exhausted from the day. I thought I would relax a little, explore some television, and then get down to prayer. I turned on the TV and clicked through the channels again and again, unable to concentrate. I thought I would read. After looking at the same page for more than half an hour, I gave that up too. I almost yelled out to God, "Okay, I will think about this now!" I began to list all the things that would have to happen for me to go to seminary, to pursue this call:

- 1. Work part-time
- 2. Sell my house

Second Sunday in Lent

- 3. Figure out how to pay for school

As I was listing all these problems to be overcome, my phone rang. It was my friend and supervisor at work, someone who never called me on Saturday. She was looking for a phone number that I gave her. Then I asked what she had been doing on her day off. She said to me, in these exact words, "I felt called to write some worship music, so that's what I have been doing today."

I related to her the conversation with my pastor, the dilemma of only being able to work part time, my concerns. I could hear the support and joy in her voice as she said, "Bonnie, you could work for us part-time forever. Don't let that stand in your way." I don't remember much of the rest of the conversation, but I had affirmed I could have a job if I decided to do this.

As I prayed that afternoon, I asked God to make a way through the rest of the stumbling blocks I had identified. It was a bargain; God, you clear the way and I'll go. Sunday morning, I went to worship and as I walked in my pastor took one look at me and said, "You've decided to do this, haven't you?" I could only nod my head yes. I would explore it, I thought.

That Sunday after worship, a young woman, new to the church, asked if I knew of a small house for sale. Her mother was moving to the area and was looking. I indicated I was thinking of selling my house. She and her husband came on Monday. I named my price. They said yes and God brought me one step closer. I looked online at the seminary schedule and saw that I was within the limit for starting in the fall. I filled out the application and scheduled an appointment with admissions. I prepared my documentation in a notebook and went in to meet with them.

Two days after my acceptance, I received a letter indicating I had received a President's Scholarship paying more than half my seminary costs. I also was notified there was a one-bedroom apartment on the grounds available to me if I wanted it. God was making the path more and more clear.

Two months before I was to begin, I got a call from the Director of the Graduate program I taught in. She said she had taken another job and was recommending me to direct the graduate program. I indicated that I was going back to school full time. She assured me that with the weekend college schedules I should be able to manage both. The salary was more than I had been making and it had full benefits. I was interviewed and got the job. God had pushed another stumbling block out of the way.

Once I stood firm in God's call for me and for my life, all the barriers, all the stumbling blocks I thought were in the way began to disappear, began to be solved. I finished seminary in three years, serving as a licensed minister my final two years. I was called to my first church during the spring of my last year. I reconciled with my husband. I was ordained, renewed my wedding vows, and moved to my first call all within a month. My new role was cemented. I had stood firm in my faith and God had stood beside me. God called me to take a bold step and once I stopped long enough to allow God to do the work in my life, I was able to identify a clearer path ahead.

I stopped focusing on what I thought I needed in my earthly life and instead began to focus on what God wanted for me, for my life. I know my call is true. I know that all the skills I gained in my secular life I brought with me into my pastoral life. It has been an amazing journey — one I could not have imagined in all those years I was arguing with God about the direction for my life.

What God is calling you to do next? Where is your ministry? What is your ministry? How do we nurture each other, our siblings in the faith, for that ministry and move into a new day in a new way?

The answers to those questions may be unclear at this moment. Prayer and discernment will lead you to the answers God has laid before you. I know the answers are there. I know the stumbling blocks can be overcome. Has my journey been easy? No, it all took hard work. Yet, focusing on God and focusing on the journey, I was called to take has made all the difference. Standing firm in the Lord has made all the difference.

I have a friend who talks about tough and challenging times using a modified cliché, "I know God never closes a door, without

Second Sunday in Lent

God opening a window, but it can become hell in the hallway." The uncertainty of what is to be of the call on our lives, to be faithful can seem a burden; but the questions you ask God, the study you undertake, the prayers you offer and share, these will help lead you to answers, help you make it through the hallway.

The Sidewalk Prophets ask us to stand firm and to never give up hope; that God has our lives in his control. Look up those lyrics online. They are comforting words. Amen.

Third Sunday in Lent

1 Corinthians 10:1-13

Seeking The Presence Of God

It is a well-known cliché that "God never gives us more than we can handle", but I have sometimes found that not to be so. When my youngest brother died of brain cancer at age five, it was more than I could handle. When my first husband was emotionally and physically abusive, it was more than I could handle. When my second husband and I lost our twin sons at birth, it was more than I could handle. The COVID pandemic was more than we could handle. Wars and violence are often more than we can handle. Homelessness, poverty, grief, and loss are often more than we can handle.

And by the way, I don't think God caused all those things to happen, short of creating us and our world, giving us free will, and allowing us to mess up on our own or collectively. Paul seems to be writing about this very thing: "God is faithful, and he will not let you be tested beyond your strength, but with the testing he will also provide the way out so that you may be able to endure it" (1 Corinthians 10:13 NRSV). I am reminded of an amendment to the cliché I first mentioned. Somewhere in my memory I think it was authored by Mother Teresa, although I cannot find the original source. The revision is, "I know that God won't give me more than I can handle. I just wish he didn't trust me so much."

I have felt that way. Haven't you? Clearly, he knew suffering and hardships. Our Hebrew ancestors did as well. Paul had some harsh things to say about how the Hebrew people utilized their connections and relationship with God. Paul recounted the sins of the people and indicated they were punished for their wrongdoing. Paul claimed they were punished as an example for

Third Sunday in Lent

us. The Israelites were indulgent, giving in to their own desires and their own will, and therefore they received punishment from God. Theologically, I am not sure I can agree with Paul. I don't think God aims a mighty finger at those who turn away from righteousness and sends plagues and punishments to individuals or groups. I think God could choose to do that, but I think God is much more concerned with calling us into communion than shunning us.

Think about it. We know what is good and right in our interactions with each other. We know that hate and anger expressed toward our neighbor hurts us almost as much as it hurts them. Think about indulging our sweet tooth. A little sweet is okay, but pampering ourselves with all the sweets we can imagine eating wrecks our health and our waistline. Seeking to follow our own path sometimes gets us in trouble with ourselves, with each other and with God. Breaking relationships through our own whim and indulgence is not really a good thing.

Somehow some of the Corinthians thought that by nature of their baptism and their continuing Holy Communion participation, they could actually do anything else they wanted. Paul used the example of the Israelites in the wilderness, identified as the chosen people, misunderstanding their role. To be chosen was not only to be set apart but was to be an example for those who have not been. It's like a pastor, a minister of the church, having to live into the ministerial code of ethics. It doesn't mean a minister might not make a mistake, but it does mean that a minister knows they are an example of one faithful to God, one set apart, and one whose example is monitored. There are expectations.

Paul reminded the people of Corinth and us that it is not good to get overconfident about our place in God's realm. It is not good to fail to set an example of one who lives exemplifying the gift of the Spirit, in faithfulness to God. No, we don't earn our way into God's grace. We have already been given grace. What we do is act according to the grace we have been given. Acting in righteousness is our way of demonstrating our gratitude for the gifts we have been given by God. We shouldn't get overconfident or overindulgent in our self-assurance, especially so much so that we no longer see God's call on our lives as the most important.

Lent is a time for reflection, introspection, and a renewing of our promises to God. Lent is a time to journey with Jesus, witnessing his service to us and his love for us. Lent is a time to grow into a deeper relationship with God and into a deeper practice of our faith. Lent is a time to seek God and to call on God for forgiveness and mercy. Lent is a time to reflect on how we are giving thanks for the grace and forgiveness as well as the presence of God in our lives.

We all have the capacity to turn to faithfulness and to be God's grace to others. The Corinthians forgot that for a little while. They focused instead on what *they* wanted, what *they* desired, and how sanctified they thought *they* had made themselves through their faith practices.

Again, we all have the capacity to turn to faithfulness and to be God's grace to others. That is our call as followers of Jesus.

"Some years ago, the noted Australian poet, Victor Daly, was dying in a Catholic hospital. One day, while he still had strength and a lucid mind, he invited the nuns who were nursing him to gather around his bed so he could express his appreciation to them for their kindness and care. After thanking them with well-chosen words, the nun who was in charge said to him, "Victor, you shouldn't thank us. You should thank the grace of God."

With the insight and the wisdom of the true poet that he was, he said to her, 'But aren't you the grace of God?'"[1]

We, too, are called to be the grace of God, to live with faithfulness, and as Paul writes, God is faithful, and he will not let you be tested beyond your strength. But with the testing he will also provide the way out so that you may be able to endure it (1 Corinthians 10:13 NRSV). God will not ask us to be more faithful than we have been given the grace to be.

There is much we are called to be and do as faithful followers of Jesus. Yet God will not really ask us for more than is possible

---

[1] Milo Thornberry , http://www.maherconsulting.com/bumc/sermondetail.cfm?ID=252.

Third Sunday in Lent

for us to give. God will equip us for whatever the demands are on our life. I mentioned before that I don't think God points a mighty finger at us and causes bad things to happen to us. I think rather, God is walking beside us, as close as our own breath, when bad or tragic things happen to us. We have two choices: we can move into the embrace of God and seek to feel deeply God's presence or we can move away from God angrily asking God why we were not spared. The choice is really ours — that is our gift, and sometimes our curse, of free will.

Bad things happen to all of us. Struggles come into the lives of most of us. None of us are spared the loss of someone we love, the illness of someone we care about. Many of us experience natural disasters and sometimes disasters of our own making. Yet, we are never alone. When we do not feel God, God has not moved away from us; more likely we have moved away from God. The question for the Jesus follower is: who do you seek in those natural and human-made disasters, in that time of pain and loss? Who do you look for? Whose strength do you rely upon?

Some years ago, I wrote a book, "*Navigating The River Of Grief.*" In it, I spoke with many people who were grieving and talked about where they encountered God in their grief. While the folks were in different stages of their grief, had very recent losses, in some cases within a few weeks, to every person they mentioned feeling the presence of God. They all, these people of faith, felt the accompaniment of God with them in their grief and loss. Many of them spoke about being angry with God, about expressing their anger toward God. That was my experience as well. Yet, these folks, and others with whom I have worked, felt the presence of God in their challenges and knew God was with them.

When have you felt the presence of God? It might have been in the whisper of a breeze on a cool day. It might have been in the hug of a child or grandchild. It may have been hearing a piece of music or a hymn that touched your spirit. It may have been in prayer or in contemplation. It might even have been in the moments when you gathered strength to face a challenge or to do a hard thing. In those moments, I personally say a silent or even a spoken prayer for strength, for understanding, for God to surround me and embrace me. You see, contrary to the old cliché, I don't think God gives us things to handle, I think God handles things with us — walks with us, talks with us, empowers and enlightens us.

It is our calling and our gift to live into our faithfulness. We are not to indulge ourselves with our self-righteousness or our individual positions of piety, rather we are to come to God, to come humble before God to gain the wisdom, the courage and the faith to step into whatever difficulties we are facing. This Lenten season, maybe we can focus a little on reflection, introspection, and a renewal of our faith promises to God. As we do so, we can ask to feel, even more clearly, God's presence with us in the hard things we encounter. Amen.

Fourth Sunday in Lent

2 Corinthians 5:16-21

A New Creation In Hope

In Christ, we are a new creation. We, each of us, have been transformed and we need to look at the world, not from the human, but from the divine perspective. What does that mean to you? Paul saw the coming of Christ as the new act of creation. Just as in Genesis, God dramatically spoke creation, our world, into being. The coming of Christ was a new creation that freed humans from bondage and moved us into the light of life. Christ was and is the new beginning of our lives in relationships to God. What was old has been washed away. We are renewed and transformed.

As faithful followers of Jesus, it is not that Jesus simply reordered the world, but that we are called into living in the risen Christ. We are called to become involved in the new transformed order created through the coming of Jesus into the world. We are transformed, renewed, and through us the world is also renewed and transformed.

We are called into the work of becoming a new creation, redeemed, and gathered. We are called to be God's own people. Just as that long-ago message written for the church in Corinth was a message of belonging to God, this message is for us as well. All the faithful, all who follow Jesus, are welcome into the reordering of the world. Everyone is welcome. Everyone is gathered in. Those who are blind to God's love and truth are gathered. Those who cannot hear God's message are gathered. Every man, woman and child is gathered, called God's own. And even more than that, God counts us on to be the witnesses of God's love, truth, mercy, patience, and of all the other blessings we receive from God.

Living in Hope

What are we doing to reorder the world, to be a part of transformation and the bringing about of the new creation? It's important to realize that the new creation, the transformation begins in our minds — our thoughts, our attitudes, our outlook on ourselves, our faith, and our world. How are we looking at the world these days? How are we seeing our role in the world?

A year or so ago, I wrote a sermon on the greatest commandments. It wasn't using this scripture as its basis but the concepts seem important to share here. If we are about the transformation of the world, we start by following the commands of our God through Christ. I asked a question about what our response to the love of God needed to be. How do we show our kinship with Jesus, change our attitudes so people know that we are children of God acting in the world? The premise of the sermon was that we love God and love people. To me, that is the transformation of our thoughts and attitudes as human beings — to move into loving God and loving people, our neighbors — all our neighbors. If we boil down all the messages about transforming the world, about being transformed through faith, that's what our faith is all about: loving God and loving people.

It's a little like the story about a man who had a huge boulder in his front yard. He grew weary of this big, unattractive stone in the center of his lawn, so he decided to take advantage of it and turn it into an object of art. He went to work on it with hammer and chisel, and chipped away at the huge boulder until it became a beautiful stone elephant. When he finished, it was gorgeous, breathtaking.

A neighbor asked, "How did you ever carve such a marvelous likeness of an elephant?"

The man answered, "I just chipped away everything that didn't look like an elephant!"

When we chip away everything else, the way we participate in the transformation of ourselves and the world is to chip away the excess, and focus on love — love from God, love to God and love shared with the world. A new humanity, a new creation, would, I believe, be a humanity and a creation built on love, celebrating love. Love births the other gifts of the spirit. Love births hope for a new way, a new creation. And because we are children of God, we are beloved, just as Jesus is beloved because he is a child of God. We enter into new life, new creation, and a new covenantal relationship with God. We are loved.

We are loved despite our flaws and failings, despite our sins. We are loved when we behave in the way God calls us to behave — when we love our neighbors as ourselves — and we are loved when we do not behave in the ways God calls us to behave — when we are angry, spiteful, and filled with prejudice and selfishness. We are loved in any case.

Yet, if we want to be a part of the reordering, the new creation, we must choose to act with mercy, compassion, kindness, and love as a means of thanking God for the wonder of our birth, our life, our blessings. We must act as one who follows Jesus, not to earn our way into God's family, but in thankfulness for our eternal inclusion in God's family. It is our way of becoming part of the transformation Paul is writing about. As we realize that Jesus is in us and we are in him, we feel and live a life intimately connected to God and to one another, marked as God's own by the love we share, by the righteousness we demonstrate, by the gratitude we express, and by the hope we know.

As we live into hope, the hope that comes from knowing we are beloved and blessed, we are called to share that hope with others — that hope the prophets proclaimed, that hope that brought Jesus into the world, that hope born in us as part of the new creation of God through Christ.

As I was preparing to write this sermon, I was listening to a song from a Christian music duo For King and Country. They are two men from Australia. I was listening to their song titled "Crave" and the lyrics of that song reminded me how much we, and the world, need hope. Look up those lyrics. They are powerful words.

Hope is what we crave — as individuals, families, and nations. Hope is what we need. Hope is God's mark on us. Hope is what we each and all can use to transform, to reorder the world into a

Living in Hope

new creation.

Hope reminds us we are never alone; we are always included. We are called, loved, nurtured, and blessed. We are gathered in and welcomed back when we have wandered away. To be marked as participants with Jesus in the new creation, in the transformation of the world is to be called to live our lives loving God with all our hearts; minds, souls and strength. To be marked as God's own is to be called to live our lives loving our neighbors — all our neighbors — whether we know them, understand them, are comfortable with them, or whether they are complete strangers with names we cannot easily say or remember, languages we do not know and customs we do not understand. To be marked as God's own is to walk in the footsteps of Jesus — offering compassion, inclusion, healing, recognition, kindness, truth, love and the hope we, and the rest of the world, crave. To be marked by God is to be transformed and to transform. Amen.

Fifth Sunday in Lent

Philippians 3:4b-14

Pressing On In Faith

Recently at the gym, working out with my personal trainer, and straining to finish the third set of an exercise, the trainer began to encourage me. "You're doing great! You can do it." As I read this portion of Paul's letter to the church of Philippi, I was reminded of this encouragement.

To many, it seems, at least at the beginning of this reading, that Paul was bragging a little. No one deserved to be more confident in his acceptance into the faith than he did. After all, he was a circumcised Jew. He was a zealous prosecutor of the faith — namely bringing Jesus' followers to the high church officials for sentencing and sometimes death. When he gave up that role and became a disciple of Jesus, Paul gave up his status with regard to the Jewish faith. It seems like a lot of self-identification is powerful and strong. Yet, Paul reminded us of his uncertainty as well. "If somehow I may attain the resurrection from the dead," he wrote. He was uncertain in that moment of whether his faithfulness was enough.

As we read, Paul accepted that his resurrection was in the hands of God. It was a result of his faith in Jesus, not in all the good works, tasks, or righteous acts he had performed. He continues, in this letter, to write that he is to press on toward the goal — and it is a goal much more difficult than my completing a set of exercises at the gym. The goal of faithfulness is challenged every day by those around us, by pain, by isolation, by the judgments of others, and our own self-judgment.

Are we pressing on? Are we resting on our faith in Jesus, seeking to strengthen it, seeking to live it in every moment of every day? Or are we resting on what we have done before?

Living in Hope

That's part of the challenge of living in a human world. How do we strengthen and deepen our faith? I know a lot of folks who seem to have a checklist. Have I prayed today? Check. Have I worshiped with my faith community this week? Check. Have I made a donation to the church? Check. But faith, my friends, is not about a checklist, a to-do list of tasks to accomplish. Rather, faith is about our relationships, our relationships with God, Jesus, and the Holy Spirit, our relationships with our siblings in faith and those without faith, our relationships with family, friends, strangers, and those we may never meet. Oh, if only being faithful was a checklist. How easy that would be!

Rather we are called to move into our relationship with God, even if we don't know if we are successful. Certainly, we should pray. Certainly, we should attend worship. Certainly, we should give to the church and to missions in the world. Yet, my friends, we do not earn our way into God's love and grace. We are freely given grace and love. We engage in spiritual practices and follow spiritual disciplines as a means of thanking God for the blessings, love, and grace we have received. There are things we need to do, but our way to faithfulness is not through doing. Our way to faithfulness is in being the people God is calling us to be, living in the path Jesus has created for us, accepting the strengthening and encouragement of the Holy Spirit, being open to all God has to offer and then being the light of those gifts in the world.

Another thing to think about as we read this passage. Paul speaks to our Lenten context of giving up or leaving behind something during the season. That is often the question, right? What are you giving up for Lent? Surely, we can give up dessert, chocolate, or maybe even meat. Does that bring us closer to God or to our neighbor? What about if we gave up hostility, prejudice, swearing, and expressing our temper negatively? Those things might bring us closer to God and closer to our neighbors. We might be getting closer to righteousness.

Suppose instead of giving up something, we added a spiritual discipline: meditation, prayer journaling, reading scripture daily, perhaps even tithing during Lent. What might change in our

Fifth Sunday in Lent

spirits? What might change in our relationship with God and with our neighbors? Our relationship with God in and through Christ changes us, moves beyond what we "deserve" because we are among the faithful. We begin to view the world in a different way, people in a different way, and even ourselves in a different way. It is not about following the "rules" or about giving up, but about adding to and becoming the person Christ calls us to be. Recognition of the gift of Jesus' life, ministry, death, and resurrection reminds us what we have a responsibility to do and to become.

We know from learning about Paul that he was a great believer, a great evangelist and worked planting churches for the perpetuation and expansion of the church. Yet, Paul wrote that he was still pressing on toward the goal. He had not arrived where he wanted to be in his faith. There was still more for him to do and be. And yet, it was not so important that he pursued God, but that he allowed God to pursue him, not righteousness from the law but righteousness from his relationship with God. Paul did not seek to cling to who he had been or what he had done. Rather Paul was in pursuit of who he would become and what he would do as a follower of Jesus, as a redeemed man of faith.

I wonder how we view our faith. There are some people I know, even some pastors, who feel they have "arrived." Their faith journey is complete. They have become what they intended to be and there is nothing left to do, nothing left to pursue. Is that what you believe? Is that how you feel about your faith; you have it and that is enough? Or do you feel that there is still a race for you to run, still more for you to press on toward in your pursuit of faithfulness? Our faith is fulfilled in the fulfillment of the life, death and resurrection of Jesus. Jesus opens the doors to our understanding how to live our faith, day by day, week by week, month by month, year by year. Without Jesus, Emmanuel God-With-Us, we can forget how very close God is to us, how very direct our relationships with Jesus is.

I have spent my life going to and being a part of faith communities. I was brought to church as a child, encouraged to receive sacraments, learned about my faith and practiced the disciplines of prayer and reading scripture. As I grew into adulthood, my faith was challenged by the theology of my faith community and faith leaders. My faith in God didn't waver, but my understanding of God as loving and grace-filled didn't seem to be reflected in that community or what I was hearing from the pulpit. In spite of that, I continued to worship, sing in worship, pray, and read scripture. Yet my heart was hungry. I knew there was more for me to do, learn, and be.

As I further explored what being faithful meant to me, I found a church home in the United Church of Christ. With its roots in both the Evangelical and Reformed churches and the Congregational Christian Churches, I recognized the grace and challenge in becoming a member of a non-doctrinal church, one that pushed me to develop my own understanding of faith, theology, and faith community. I began to understand what it meant to name Jesus as the head of the church and explore the ancient creeds, not as edicts, but as experiences of the faithful, seeking an understanding of deep theological truths. I was no longer limited by the doctrine someone else defined for me, but rather was encouraged to explore what faithfulness meant in covenantal relationships, which required deep listening and experiencing. I have now been a United Church of Christ member more than half my life; a United Church of Christ pastor for more than fifteen years. I still learn more about myself, my faith, and my community almost every day.

This experience helps me understand Paul's need to press forward. He was hungry for more — more experiences of God, more knowledge of his faith, and more encounters with the living Christ, the resurrected Christ. It was not his history, but his future that compelled him. It was not his exploration of God but God's exploration of him that moved him into finding deeper meaning in his faith.

What have been your experiences of faith and faith community? Do you feel nurtured or shut down? Do you feel comfortable in asking life-changing questions, having doubts,

Fifth Sunday in Lent

wondering where God is in your life? Are you resting on what you have been taught, what you have memorized and what is defined by others? Is there a willingness to learn more about how God is interacting with you and impacting your life? Are you pressing on as Paul was pressing on to become more Christlike, more in concert with God's will for your life?

Paul, the great evangelist, began to change after his Damascus Road experience with the living Christ. His life was never the same. Although he was shunned by many of his former Jewish friends, although he was arrested, scourged, and exiled, he came to know God in new and profound ways. He came to understand the God of grace, the Christ of redemption, and the power of the Holy Spirit. He planted churches of believers across Asia Minor. He blessed the churches and us with letters exploring faith, and his relationship with God, his desire to be even more attuned to God's will for his life. He pressed on. We, my friends, can do no less. Amen.

Liturgy of the Passion / Sixth Sunday in Lent

Philippians 2:5-11

Love Lives

My friends, as we gather this Sunday to recall the passing of the weeks of Lent and move ourselves into the holiest of weeks in the Christian calendar, there is no better passage for us to reflect upon. Many scholars believe this passage from the letter to the church in Philippi may have been an ancient, early Christian hymn unfolding the stages of Christ's whole being — from being in the form of God, to becoming human, to surrendering to humiliation and death, and then to ascension back into heaven. Much of Christian theology rests in these verses. Let us explore them a little and then reflect on their meaning for us in this time and place.

Paul reminds us, as does the first chapter of the gospel of John, that Jesus, being in the form of God was at the beginning, was always divine from the beginning of time, or maybe more correctly written, before the beginning of time. Jesus, as God, was and is and will be. Divinity was never in question. Jesus is God. As we move into verse seven, we find an emptying of Jesus' self so that he, as did the others in his time, became slaves to the ravages of humanity and the oppression of Rome, became fully human, encountering all that it meant.

From being born in a stable to parents with whom he became a refugee, to working with his family as a carpenter and then moving into his role as preacher, teacher, and minister to the people, Jesus was fully human. Yet, for Jesus, this was not the end. He humbled himself even further to be arrested and scourged. And as if that humiliation were not enough, he surrendered himself to be crucified and hung on a cross like a criminal.

That was not to be the end, however. From the cross he was

Liturgy of the Passion / Sixth Sunday in Lent

raised, resurrected from the dead, and given authority so that at the mention of his name, all on earth and in heaven will bow. His divinity and his humanity, were both assured, both celebrated. The whole earth is called to acknowledge the humanity and the divinity of Jesus as this brings glory to our Creator God as well.

I wonder if this passage would be a good passage to use with new Christians and church school classes to summarize, as a beginning class, the life, ministry, death, and resurrection of Jesus. Surely, each verse can be expanded to connect with the Christ story, can be expanded by other texts, and can help us explore all the teachings of Jesus. It is, however, a succinct description of the actions of God in the redemption of the world.

What does this passage say to you in this time and place, about your faith, about your understanding of Jesus? From the first, there was misunderstanding and confusion about the duality of Jesus. How could one be both God and human? It is beyond human understanding. To accept that Jesus is God is key. Jesus is the word as described in John's gospel. "In the beginning was the Word, and the Word was with God, and the Word was God" (John 1:1 NRSV). Jesus was, is, and always will be, just as God was, is, and will be. There is no separating the son from the Father, no difference, save that Jesus took a new step and became Emmanuel, God-with-us. As Paul wrote, Jesus gave up his equality with God and emptied himself to become a human being — subject to pain, illness, hostility, and even death. I, for one, have always been amazed at the depth of love that brought God to live among us and to experience our existence. It is a sacrifice I cannot imagine.

Many of us can recount sacrifices we have made for family, friends, our work companions, our faith communities, but none of us began as divine beings. We, having been born human, can understand the humanity of Jesus but cannot begin to fathom the humility for a God to come to live among us and become one of us. In this time of the creation of Marvel Comics movies with Thor, Odin, and Loki, we can imagine the power of a God — but can we imagine the humility of God to say: I will wholly become one of you, subject to all the pain and trial you experience? It is beyond my imagining. Is it beyond yours?

That is perhaps why there were so many theological debates about the divinity and humanity of Jesus. Perhaps he was wholly human but given divinity as a response to his selflessness and faith. I have heard that, haven't you? Perhaps he was wholly divine and did not really experience true humanness. I have heard that, haven't you? But to acknowledge both the divinity and the humanity of Jesus, to accept that Jesus chose to experience all of our humanity, is to accept the mystery of God and incarnation. This is difficult for some of us, easier for others. For some it seems unprovable, and yet, for me, that is what faith is about — accepting that which I cannot completely prove or understand but seeking to accept as the power of God.

The presence of Jesus among the people as preacher, teacher, healer, leader, and sanctifier is clear in all our New Testament, Christian scripture writings. Jesus born of Mary and Joseph in Bethlehem. Clearly remembered and documented. The presence of shepherds and wise men, magi, from the east were also documented. The refugee status of the family as they fled to Egypt, was documented. Much of the childhood of Jesus was undocumented, except for discussing God and the law with the leaders of the church in Jerusalem. This humble boy with such great wisdom felt a call to serve and teach in "his Father's" house, which was such a gift and such a wonder. The beginning of the public ministry of Jesus with his baptism at the River Jordan, was well documented as were his trials and temptations in the desert.

The most documented, for us was the life and active ministry, the three years when Jesus walked throughout Israel and Judah teaching people about a loving God who wanted a relationship with the people, wanted to love people more than judge them. The parables and stories, the healing, and praying, the miracles in our midst throughout the public ministry of Jesus, these were well-documented and gave us a peek at the loving character of God. The acceptance of those on the outside of the society, those who were shunned and marginalized was a key component of

Liturgy of the Passion / Sixth Sunday in Lent

Jesus' public ministry. But there was also anger — the turning over of the money-changers' tables, the naming as hypocrites the leaders of the church, more concerned with their status and the letter of the law than with the Spirit of God and God's love for the least among us. Jesus was not afraid to speak the truth — in anger and in love — in a desire to have people turn away from human status and sinfulness toward God.

This preacher and teacher, this miracle-worker, the Son of God accepted the fact that a sacrifice was needed to reconnect the people with their God. This sacrifice was his to make, his to choose, and his to accept. What other God would allow themselves to be betrayed by one of their closest friends, to be arrested and whipped, to be ridiculed and spat on, and then finally to be sentenced to death, the death of a criminal on a cross? I cannot imagine the anguish of this man, this Son of God, as he chose to accept this fate for the good of us all. Can you?

I have sometimes chosen to put myself out in the world as an object of some criticism and scorn for what, I believe, are the teachings of Christ. But I do not know if I, as a human being, would have the strength to sacrifice my life for others. I do not know if, as a parent, I could sacrifice my child for others. Yet, such is the depth of the love of Jesus, the love of God in our midst. It is key that we remember this sacrifice when we are faced with the need to stand up for our faith, to face the scorn of others for expressing that which we believe.

And yet, our hope lives, for the death is not the end. Jesus seeking forgiveness for those who were killing him speaks to reconciliation beyond my imagination. Jesus dying for you and for me is beyond my understanding. Jesus loving that much is more than I can know, or perhaps ever feel in my own life. Our hope comes from the love of God that raised Jesus from the dead, that conquered death for all time. This is the hope we have been given. This is the reason why we bow at the name of Jesus, why we follow him and strive to become more and more Christlike in our own lives. We are not lost. Death is not the end. We will be with God at the end of our human existence.

Living in Hope

This is the celebration portion of this text. God raised Jesus high so we could know the power of love, so we could speak the power of love.

When my eldest grandson was four, then living with only his mother's family (who were not believers) as she and my son had divorced, he called me with the deepest of theological questions. "Grandma Bonnie, how and why did Jesus die, and how'd he get to be alive again?" How does one answer those questions for a four-year old? I told him that Jesus came to change the world, to help people learn to love one another. Some people did not want that to happen. They wanted power and to be able to judge others. Jesus told them it was not okay, and they were so angry they decided he was dangerous, and they needed to kill him.

"Okay, grandma, but how did he get to be alive again?" I told him that God loved him so much, because Jesus was his son and God loved us so much because we are also God's children, that God could not allow his death to stand. God wanted to show the people in power and the people who had been listening to Jesus that Jesus was teaching the right things about God. So, God loved him back to life.

That seemed to settle the question for him. He knew love and he knew love was powerful. He knew I would tell him the truth, so his four-year old questions were answered. And although those answers are simplistic, they are true. Jesus loved and loves us too much to let the letter of the law rather than the love of God and people win. God loved and loves us so much that the living Christ is essential to our ongoing relationship with God and one another. Hate, anger, fear, and death could not be allowed to win. Love wins, always. Love wins.

This writing from Paul related, in very compact and simple terms, the life, death, resurrection, and ascension of Jesus. This writing from Paul reminds us that God loves us so very much that God's son, Jesus, needed to come into our midst as one of us humans and teach us how to be in relationship with God and with each other. That is our blessing. That is our faith. How will you live out your faith in Jesus today and in the days to come?

Liturgy of the Passion / Sixth Sunday in Lent

That is the question on my mind. Can it be the question on yours? Amen.

Maundy Thursday

1 Corinthians 11:23-26

At The Table

In my faith tradition, Maundy Thursday usually involved a remembrance of the first communion service. Many of the churches I have been associated with have scheduled a light supper and following that supper, at small tables of six to eight attendees, bread is broken and the cup is shared, much as this passage from 1 Corinthians related. The commemoration is somewhat solemn often because we Christians forget that this offering of bread and cup was offered during a family celebration, a Passover feast, recounting the escape of the Israelites from Egypt. It was a warm and welcoming celebration of a time that had hardships, but led to great joy.

The recounting of this first communion meal is a continuation of the meal and feasts Jesus had shared all throughout the land — sometimes with the rich and powerful, sometimes with the ostracized and marginalized — but there was power and grace in coming together at table. Perhaps that is why so many of our family celebrations take place at tables. We cannot discount the power in gathering together.

Ages ago, my sister and I were speaking about our mother. Even when there was little to share, Mom would welcome guests at the table. We lived in a fairly small home, but one Christmas Mom opened the table to the family and fourteen guests visiting from Turkey. There truly was no room, but we didn't notice. The hospitality was evident, the joy at the feast was clearly expressed. There was no room at the table, but plenty of room in our hearts. My sister wasn't even born yet, so she didn't know that story. However, there were myriad stories to choose from.

My Dad even made a joke of the hospitality, "Put more water

Maundy Thursday

in the soup. Company's coming." We'd laugh but we knew how true this was. There was always room for more. Everyone was welcome. All could join the feast and the celebration. My sister and I could recount the many times that people came to sit at our kitchen table and talk with my parents, share their lives, and sometimes even seek advice. We talked about writing a book titled *Kitchen Table Wisdom*, but neither of us has done that yet. There is still time. I can still recall the smells coming from the kitchen, the baking and cooking, the making do with less so we could share with someone else. That sense of hospitality was ingrained in us and it has become our practice as well.

Something amazing happens when people gather at the table and share one with another. Perhaps that is part of the power of the communion table and the invitation to it. All are welcome. All are invited. On the night this passage commemorates, Jesus invited to his table the one who would betray him, the one who would deny him, and the ones who would desert him. None of that mattered. All were welcome. All were called to the table to share in the feast of love, the feast bread and cup, the feast of remembrance.

There was a time when many of our churches didn't welcome those we didn't know to our communion tables. How could we be sure they had been baptized, had seen Jesus as their Savior? There were and still are times when children were excluded from the communion feast. They couldn't understand, people said, or there was a rite of passage children needed to undertake. Jesus said no such thing. In fact, Jesus is known to have said, "Bring the little children to me." How could Jesus want them to be omitted from participation at table?

The Passover celebration was a family feast, one where children have a special part to play. Children spend time at the Passover feast looking for the *afilkomen*, the piece of matzah which has been broken in two with one part hidden. This is said to be symbolic of the ultimate redemption of suffering at the end of the Passover Seder meal. It is also seen as the putting aside of something for the poor and a sign that there is more to discover in the world and in our life than we will ever know. The children have an important role in the feast; they could and should have an important role in the communion feast as well.

In a church I served, the children were not allowed to receive from the communion table until they were confirmed, in the seventh or eighth grade. In the interim teaching time, I prepared a table just for them, an Agape feast, where they could come to receive a blessing plus receive a cracker and grapes. As we moved into the educational discussion about why children couldn't participate, it became clear that tradition was the primary reason, for none of us truly understood the mystery of the presence of the risen Christ in communion. It was determined that the parents could decide when the children were ready and that I would speak with the children about the sacrament before they received the first time.

I wish I could share with you the looks of wonder and love on the faces of children when they came forward to receive communion for the first time. They may not have understood all the significance, but they knew they were encountering God, something precious and special to them. Tears came into my eyes as I served them, calling them each by name, just as Jesus calls us by name.

That is the gift of this feast. All are invited to experience the gifts and blessings of the risen Christ. The bread and cup are shared by Jesus with all present, with each and every one. Sometimes it is hard to feel worthy of that gift. I think that was the case with the disciples as well. How could Jesus be offering his body and blood for us? What depth of love was that? How could I be worthy of that sacrifice, that much redemption and love?

Recently, a contemporary Christian song has been recorded that speaks to our sense of unworthiness and Christ's continuing invitation. It's by the Sidewalk Prophets and titled "Come to the Table." The lyrics are online and you may look them up. It talks about finding grace, especially when we need it the most.

Clearly those lyrics remind us each that nothing can keep us

Maundy Thursday

from the mercy of God, nothing can keep us from the welcome of the Savior.

As we focus on this Holy Week, this holiest of weeks, who are those we are excluding from our tables? Who are the others that are unwelcome in our midst? To whom do we fail to say, "Come to the table"?

Is it the person of color, tacitly welcomed but really feared or misunderstood? Is it the divorced woman or man, who we view as a sinner and unwelcome? Is it the single mother living in poverty, who has never been married and is struggling? Is it the homeless person we often see begging on the streets with a sign who smells when he sits next to us? Is it the gay, lesbian, bisexual, or transgender person whose life we cannot begin to understand or we are unwilling to understand and affirm that it is kept from the table?

My friends, if Jesus did not exclude from the table the ones who would hurt him and abandon him to arrest, scourging, and death; why do we think it is okay for us to exclude anyone from Christ's invitation to the table? How can we determine that the Bread of Life, broken for us all, is it not for all the persons we judge as unworthy? What if those individuals judged us as unworthy?

Some of the most profound spiritual experiences of my life have been at the communion table. As a United Church of Christ pastor, I have encountered churches who receive communion at the altar rail, at the altar through intinction, have been served the elements in their pews, and have supped together at small tables sharing with one another — all breaking bread and sharing cup together. The methodologies change. The offerings of bread, through type and form, have changed. The cup has changed, either juice or wine, depending on the tradition. The Spirit is the same. The host of the feast is the same. We are invited to partake of this meal because Jesus invited us, because Jesus' body was broken for us, because Jesus' blood was poured out for us. This is his meal, his table, his invitation. The invitation is no more poignantly offered than it is on Maundy Thursday as Jesus gathered with his friends, knowing he was about to be arrested

Living in Hope

and crucified, knowing this was all necessary because human beings don't know how to reconcile themselves with God and need his intercession.

When you partake of this meal on this day, or on any other day, please remember, this table is a gift. This table is a welcome. This table is the hospitality of the one who came to live, teach, heal, die, and rise so we could be in relationship with God and with one another. Remember the sanctity and the celebration of this moment, this encounter with the risen Christ. Remember Jesus asked of us, "Whenever you share it, remember me." Amen.

Good Friday
Hebrews 10:16-25

We Build The Tomb

All my life I have struggled with the concept of calling this day of Jesus' arrest and crucifixion as "good." What could possibly be good about Jesus being arrested, tried, convicted, and crucified? How can we call this feast day "good"?

Yet, there is a reassurance for us in these words written to the Hebrew Christians. Much as the prophet Jeremiah told the Jewish people that God's law would be inscribed on their hearts, just as it was once inscribed by God's own hand on stone tablets, this letter reminds us that God's law is inscribed on our hearts through the living out of the law by Jesus. God's will lives in us through the life, ministry, and sacrifice of Jesus. We know it, we feel it, we practice this, our faith, through the leadership of Jesus. This is good. The arrest, trial, sentencing, and crucifixion of Jesus may not feel good, but the resulting forgiveness and grace, the resulting redemption certainly is.

We have been redeemed. We have been saved. Through the actions of Jesus, we are in a deeper and more substantial connection with God and with each other. Perhaps this is the good we mention when we talk about this day, it is the resulting grace and forgiveness we receive that is good. It is not the crucifixion that is good. It is not the betrayal and death of Jesus that is good but who we are able to become, how we are able to be in relationship with God, that is good.

The reassurance of the prophets and the writer of Hebrews is truly there, but there is also a reminder. Even with the words of the law inscribed on our hearts, we are still human. We still fall into the trap of sin. We may be God's own, but we sometimes forget that and we act as though our covenant with God does not exist. Let's look at some history to acknowledge how far we sometimes are from righteousness.

We could go back further, but let's start with the church in the United States. There was great debate among Christians as to whether or not the genocide of the indigenous peoples was the destiny of the white Christians who settled in what is now known as America. America was not discovered by these European folks, for indigenous people were already living and thriving here. Yet, in our move to evangelize and proselytize to the native peoples, we all but wiped out their culture their heritage their faith in the God they knew. We ripped their children from them (much as was more recently done with the children of immigrants), sent them to American boarding schools, and tried to turn them into good "European" Christians. Surely this hatred of the "weaker", the "unknown", and the people we marginalized was not consistent with the call to love God and love our neighbors.

If we move ahead but a few years, we can see the beginnings of the slave trade in the new settlements soon to be the United States. We determined that by virtue of skin color, foreign language, foreign culture, and our strength over people that we could buy and sell them like livestock. We could abuse them and separate them from their families and call them each two-thirds of person. There were those among us who used the Bible, the word and law of God, to support these practices. And even when legislation and amendments to the constitution made it illegal to buy and sell people, we found ways to continue berating, enslaving, and abusing people simply based on the color of their skin and their ancestry. Surely these practices were not consistent with the call of God to love God and to love our neighbors.

We can continue to cite example after example of the sins of our culture, or to mention the individual sins we commit: lying, adultery, violence, hate, theft — the lists would become too long to imagine. Yet, we have the law written and etched on our hearts. We call ourselves and are called to be people of God. We, in spite of the gift of the law, the redemption of Jesus, are sinning human beings. We can still perform lawless deeds with the law written

Good Friday

on our hearts.

Even though the words of God, the law, is etched on our hearts, it still has to be lived out with our hearts. We still need to come into connection with the law written within us in our everyday actions and our everyday interactions with one another. Jesus reminded us that the thought of the sin, the attitude of the sin, is as egregious as the sin itself. Thus it is our attitude that we need to change, that we need to continually re-center on God. It is in our hearts that the divine will of God and the human will intersect.

I don't know about you, but I recognize that my thoughts are sometimes more human than faithful. When I am driving and I am cut off in traffic or I am following an exceptionally slow driver (I seem to always be in a hurry), I am less than loving. If alone in the car, I sometimes even verbally attack the other driver. Surely not a Christian act of a Christian heart.

There is still a tendency, although I have largely overcome it, to deny a mistake or a failing, not lying exactly but avoiding blame that creeps into my mind before I admit my mistake. Surely that is not the most honest approach and not a Christian act of a Christian heart.

Yet I know that if I accept that I have sinfulness in my heart, I can also accept the forgiveness that comes through the acts of Jesus, through the love of God. When our actions are at odds with the call of God on our lives, with the law God has written in our hearts, we seek forgiveness. That forgiveness, for us Christians, is mediated through the life and death, the sacrifice of Jesus. We can make our own offerings of recompense to the one we have wronged, but forgiveness comes from God, comes through God.

For what have you sought forgiveness this Lenten season? Who has been the brunt of our anger, your lack of consideration, your selfishness or greed? With whom do you need to make peace and amends? We can forgive and we can ask to be forgiven because God first offered forgiveness to us. We know how we feel when we forgive. It is, after all, more about us than the one we are forgiving. To fail to forgive provides us with one more burden to carry, one more stone in the wall between us and another. This is not God's hope for us.

One Lent, when I was serving in a local congregation, we built the tomb of Jesus during our prayers of confession. Each of us was given a roughhewn stone on our way into worship. Each Sunday during the silent prayer of confession, we walked to the front of the sanctuary with our stone and laid it on the stone cave, the tomb in which Jesus would be buried on Good Friday. The silent procession was powerful as each member thought about one or more sins they needed to confess before God. We each came forward with the knowledge that our sinfulness separates us from God and from one another. Each stone added to the size and weight of the tomb in which our Savior would be buried.

On Good Friday, we draped the edges of the table and the tomb in black. We took all the other ornamentation, all other symbols of our faith: the cross, the baptismal font, the candles, the Bible, everything off the chancel as we stripped it bare. Only the tomb, the large stone tomb draped in black remained as we left the sanctuary in silence, recognizing the separation our sin has caused, the pain for ourselves and for others. This recognition of our sinfulness was good. Our hearts were opened to our humanity, our sin, and left open for God to fill.

God, as we know, does not leave us in our despair, in our separation from God. Rather, God opens the gates of love, grace, forgiveness, and heaven to us through the sacrifice of Jesus. Jesus provides us direct access to God and to God's all-embracing love and forgiveness. Jesus unlocks the doors, breaks down the walls we have built which separate us from God. The writer of Hebrews provides us with hope. When our hearts truly seek God, God is present; God is faithful. When we cannot succeed on our own, we are reminded to hold fast to the promises of God.

More than that, we are called to community, to attend meetings with the faithful, to encourage each other, and to spur one another toward love and good deeds. We certainly can worship God, align our minds and hearts with God, when we are alone. Yet, there is something about community that strengthens

Good Friday

us, that helps us focus on what is true, what is real, and what is everlasting. Jesus could have done all his ministry alone, but we humans cannot. Jesus built a community of faithful followers so when he was no longer physically present with them, they could encourage one another and support one another in living into their faithfulness. They supported one another as Jesus was arrested, tried and crucified. They supported each other after the crucifixion and later after the resurrection and ascension. They supported each other in the ways we are called to support one another in our faithfulness, in our striving to live the law that is engraved on our hearts.

That opening of the doors to heavenly forgiveness, our redemption, and our sanctification, are the things that make this a good day, Good Friday. It is not the earthly occurrences, but the heavenly ones that make the day good. Through the earthly actions of those who took the life of Jesus, we are redeemed. We are reconnected with the law written on our hearts.

That tomb we built with our sin in that church I served — on Easter, the stones were rolled away and revealed an empty tomb. Our Lord had risen. We had been forgiven. Our sins, just like the stones, had been removed. Amen.

Resurrection of the Lord

1 Corinthians 15: 19-26

We Live In Hope

Good morning! Christ is risen! Christ is risen indeed! Happy Easter!

Several times this week I have revised this sermon message, wanting to incorporate the emotions of this Holy Week, to understand the last week as a journey with Jesus and the disciples. The joy and triumph of Palm Sunday quickly seems to move into the intimacy of Maundy Thursday with its meal shared among friends, the servant leader Jesus washing the feet of his disciples, and the breaking of bread and sharing of cup. We then quickly move to the pain and suffering of Good Friday, of the betrayal, arrest, torture, crucifixion, and death. And then it was Saturday.

All day Saturday, I wondered how the disciples spent their day. They were in the in-between time, the time between the loss of their beloved friend and teacher, and their true understanding of Christ's return in three days. They must have been sad. They must have been looking back at the last years wondering if they could have done something to prevent the crucifixion, wondering if this was truly God's plan, and wondering about that Passover meal and the prayers they could have, and perhaps should have, said in the garden that night.

Reverend Doctor Mark Miller, who served as the transitional interim minister of the Pacific Northwest Conference of the United Church of Christ is known for saying, "Your windshield needs to be larger than your rearview mirror." I know that the disciples didn't have windshields and rearview mirrors, but Jesus was trying to teach them the same thing by saying to a would-be disciple, "No one who puts a hand to the plow and looks back is fit for the kingdom of God."

Resurrection of the Lord

I wonder what Jesus thought of all the looking back the disciples were doing. And I wonder how much of it was sharing memories and how much of it was wishing for the day before, the minute before, when Jesus was still with them. I wonder if Peter wished he would have a chance to apologize, or if they were mourning Judas, his betrayal, and his loss. I wonder if they thought about arguing over who should be first and whether or not they could drink from the cup from which Jesus had drunk.

They would have celebrated the sabbath as well — although celebrate would be a strong word. They would have prayed the *Shema, Sh'ma Yis'ra'eil Adonai Eloheinu Adonai echad*: Hear, Israel, the Lord is our God, the Lord is one. *Barukh sheim k'vod malkhuto l'olam va'ed*: Blessed be the name of his glorious kingdom forever and ever.

It would have been difficult to praise God that day just as difficult as it is for us to praise God in times of sorrow, illness, loss, or pain. It is challenging to lift up our praise to God when we do not understand why things are going wrong in our lives or in the world. But we, just as the disciples, or maybe even more so because we know how the story ends, are called to believe in the power and presence of our God, and to praise God for all the blessing and challenges we have.

How do we explain the resurrection of Jesus? Can we? Perhaps not. Yet, the resurrection of Jesus is the foundation of our faith, of the Christian faith. If there is no resurrection, there is no Christianity. The essence of this Easter celebration is the resurrection, the conquering of death by our God. To deny this, even if we cannot explain it, is to lose the essence of what it means to be Christian, what it means to be a Jesus follower. We may never know how it happened. We may debate what it means, yet, we each believe firmly that God conquered death. That is the essence of being a Christian: Christ is risen.

You may recall from an earlier message that my eldest grandson once asked me, "How and why did Jesus die and how did he get to be alive again?" My response to him, at least about the resurrection, was that love raised Jesus from the dead. The love of God for his son and for humanity raised Jesus from the dead. It was much harder to explain to him a mere five years later why his mother died and why his prayers for her resurrection (at least so that he could see and touch her) were not answered. How do you explain to a child that his mother was, in fact, raised from the dead but not to walk on the earth, but to be with God in heaven? Complex questions that are beyond my ability to explain to a nine-year old. He is eighteen now and still has more questions than answers, including whether or not there is a God. His confusion is not solitary. He understands there is one larger and more powerful than he, but does not view God in the ways some people of faith do — he is not a conservative and he does not believe in the puppeteer God that controls every action. He is put off by the people who proclaim he is going to heal because he does not believe in God, as they define God to him.

Rather, he asks questions about this godhead, this almighty being who created all that is and loves his children enough to let them have free will and mess the world up until it has gotten to the state it is in. He has faith that there is more to life than what he can see, touch, taste, and smell, but he hasn't quite figured out the nature of God in his own experience. He knows love. He feels love. He knows forgiveness. He feels forgiveness. He has long theological conversations with me, but more questions than answers and I will admit, I do not have all the answers either.

Do I know the actions required of God to have raised Jesus from the dead? No, I do not. Do I believe with all my heart that Jesus is risen? Yes, I do. I do not have to be able to define it, to structure the process, to believe that the living Christ is present. I have seen and experienced his presence, heard his voice, and felt his touch. Some of you may remember when I shared the story of encountering Jesus while being guided through a meditation, as a part of the spiritual exercises of Saint Ignatius. As I was walking into the dark, dank basement I was using as a symbol for my sinfulness, I saw a light and as the light came closer a figure became clearer. I know, without a doubt in my being, that this was Jesus reaching out to me. Jesus spoke, "Come" and extended

Resurrection of the Lord

his arms to me. It wasn't until Jesus came another step closer and again spoke, "Come" that I raced into his embrace. I knew the presence of the risen Christ, forgiving and loving me, in a way I could never, had never, and have never known it again. Yet, of all the readings and studying and learning about Christianity I have done, this one experience is the certainty on which my belief in the resurrection rests. I do not know how, but I know it to be so.

Paul shared his certainty in the resurrection with us, but went even further. Not only is Christ risen, but we will all be risen in Christ as well. This is the belief with which I spoke with certainty to my grandson about his mother's resurrection. This is the certainty with which Paul wrote to the church in Corinth.

How can this be? Well, Paul uses an ancient belief, that humans were once divine and then fell into sinfulness as the example for us. If the actions of one he named Adam can result in the fall into sinfulness as all human beings, how much more likely is it that the resurrection of one, Jesus, Son of God, can result in the resurrection of us all? Genesis 1-3 reminds us of the fall into sinfulness. The Easter gospel reminds us of the resurrection of Jesus. Our destiny is defined by both, not only by one.

I have written before about my own sinfulness and admitted that sometimes my attitudes are not as God would wish. I also can rest on the forgiveness of God through Jesus — my vision and experience of Jesus affirms that for me. Through my sinfulness I "die", and through God's forgiveness and Jesus' resurrection, I live.

How assured are you of your destiny in faith? Have you thought much about what brings you toward sin and what moves you back into relationship with God? This day of all Christian days, we can celebrate the certainty that we are forgiven, redeemed, and undeniably connected to the salvation of being in Christ. Easter is the good news of all the Christian faith. Through the resurrection of Jesus, we have the hope, no the certainty, that the resurrection is also for us. Death had been defeated for all time.

Have you ever been at the bedside of one who is actively

Living in Hope

dying? There are machines, people, prayer, and grief. There is the essence of the living person struggling either to live or to die. You can, if you are intuitive, feel the presence, the spirit, the essence of the person who is lying in bed awaiting death. I have sat at many such bedsides. I can feel the pain of the relatives in the room. Sometimes I can feel the pain of the person who is dying. I can sometimes even feel the presence of God as I anoint the dying and pray for and with that person and those they leave behind. As the person moves into death, takes perhaps a last gasping breath, or simply ceases to breathe, there is, in the room, a difference. Before machines beep and people are visibly aware, sometimes there is simply a shift in the energy, the soul of the person leaves them, leaves us, and moves on to God. This is a resurrection moment, a moment when death is defeated, not by the body, but by the soul, by the spirit which has gone home. It is a profound moment and a profound experience for a pastor to feel and know the soul lives on with God, not with the body. I am not sure anyone who has not experienced this, and even those of us who have, can describe it well. Yet, I know it to be so. Death had been defeated. Resurrection came. That is the message of Easter. Our future, as Christ followers, as disciples of Jesus, is life, not death. All life has within it the possibility of resurrection. Death has been conquered.

Martin Luther said, "Our Lord Jesus has written the promise of the resurrection, not in the books alone but in every leaf of springtime." This is the message for us at Easter. Resurrection comes! God and God's love wins! We are both redeemed in the here and now, and into the future into an eternal future that, without Easter, we could not imagine. We are undeniably linked to Christ through our faith in him, through our emulation of him in our everyday lives, and finally in our resurrection through the door he has opened for us. May we know that joy this day and in all the days yet to come. We are Easter people. We are resurrection people. We live! Amen.

Second Sunday of Easter
Revelation 1:4-8

Visions Of Hope

Welcome to the second Sunday of Easter. Yes, my friends, Easter is not simply a feast day, it is a season of the celebration of the resurrection of Jesus. There is much to learn and to explore between now and the beginning of Pentecost, the next liturgical season to arrive in our calendars.

We begin this Sunday with a passage from the New Testament book of Revelation, the Revelation of John, which can be one of the most difficult books to understand and interpret. Once, when asked how I interpreted the book, without meaning to be funny or facetious, countered, "Which interpretation: theologically, politically, historically, or metaphorically?" I could have added many more forms of interpretation, but those were the ones that came to my mind initially. I suppose writings about visions are almost always difficult to understand.

Luckily, this passage is relatively easy to interpret, as interpretations go. We know that John was writing to seven churches, his churches, as their pastor. He wanted to share with them his wisdom, insights, and one presumes, pastoral care while he was in exile. There was triumph and hope in this passage. He offered his parishes peace and hope — peace and hope from God, Jesus, and the Holy Spirit. There is strength in these words, a positive focus, a renewal of hope in the omnipresent God. John wrote with acclamation for Jesus, the faithful one, the firstborn of the dead who with God would reign in glory forever, and the ruler of all kings of the earth. The preeminence of Jesus was clear. He was one, the most faithful one, who witnessed to the love of God even to his own death. Jesus was the first to be raised from the dead, resurrected to reign in glory with God forever. Jesus was the one with power over all earthly kings; he was exalted above all others.

John was affirming to us that those who follow in the way of Jesus will likewise remain faithful, be resurrected, and be joined with God, Jesus, and the Holy Spirit in the realm of God. There was deep hope in this; an abiding hope shared with the churches from which John had been removed and exiled. The people were not alone. Cling to the faith — follow in the footsteps of Jesus. God is in control.

And it is not just the present time in which God has control. Utilizing the first and last letters of the Greek alphabet, John accented that God is the beginning and the end, always was and always is. God is both the author and the keeper of time in an absolute sense. This harkens us back to the Old Testament reading of Exodus here when asked who God was, God revealed, *"I am who I am"* (Exodus 3:14). There is no doubt that God is, was, and always will be. John reminded us that God is the source of all that is, all human experience flows out of the creative and creating power of God.

John did not just speak of the past and the present time. John spoke with the knowledge of the eschatology, with a vision of the coming of Jesus that reminds us of the prophet Daniel. This future in which Christ returns to earth, comes amidst the clouds in a way that every eye will see him, and will know him to be the Christ. God, through Christ, will have the last word for all humanity, for everything created. This vision of the world, this future second coming of Jesus, will encompass all the world. All will know Christ. All will see Christ. All will experience Christ, even those who pierced him — the oppressors from Rome and the hierarchy of the Jewish faith who colluded with them, will know Christ.

These are powerful images. Images that align the followers of Jesus, oft persecuted, imprisoned and killed, with a future defined by Jesus, ruled and manifested through Jesus. Imagine being the most oppressed of people, your pastor arrested and exiled, and receiving a message of hope that professes that the best is yet to

Second Sunday of Easter

come. Jesus is coming. God is coming. We, the faithful, will be redeemed and triumph. It's like magnifying the underdog team's victory over their opponent by hundreds. Our pain is not in vain. Our faithfulness pays off. We, in the end, will win.

Have you ever been on a team that wasn't expected to fare very well? When I was a senior in high school, the high school boys challenged the high school girls to a soccer game. Even though we spoke out of confidence, we were pretty sure we girls would lose. Yet, we faced the challenge. We played our hearts out. The boys who were a little overconfident, didn't start out taking us very seriously. Ultimately, we girls won. We cheered and celebrated and I have to admit, even bragged a little. It was as if we had been told we were good enough.

Another story shared by my sister: When she was in high school, the football team was really good. They won a regional title the previous year and were expected to go all the way to the state finals during that season. However, the coach discovered the whole first string had been to a party and had been drinking. All of them were underage and this was a violation of their code as players. At the next practice, the whole first string was benched. They were told they would be required to come to all practices and all games, but they would not be allowed to play. The second string would play the remainder of the season. You can imagine the uproar. They had the chance to win the championship. How could the coach do this? Didn't he care about having a winning season? The second string persevered. They practiced harder than ever before. Even when the stands were empty because people were angry with the coach, the boys played their hearts out. At the end of the season when the second string captain held the state championship trophy, there was not a dry eye in the stadium or in the school the following weeks. They had done it. Their hard work and faith had paid off. Doing the right thing was rewarded.

This is the kind of message John was sending to the churches. Keep the faith. Hang on to hope. God is with us. Jesus will come again. We are loved. We are freed from our sins. Jesus has done

Living in Hope

that for us. We now are called to be priests on God's behalf. There is power in that kind of message and in John's belief in his churches, in Jesus' belief in his followers.

And yet there is a message, a warning about the future, perhaps it is even a threat against those who have caused his exile on Patmos. "All the people on the earth will mourn because of him." Some translations read, "All the peoples of the world shall lament in remorse" (REB). There will be difficult times ahead. There will be mourning, lament, and weeping. There will be a need for repentance and forgiveness. The message is both a warning and message. Remain faithful and know you are redeemed. Those who threaten will also lament and need forgiveness. There are the beloved of God and those who ignore God. One group will find peace and the other will mourn.

The message is clear. Come into, and stay in relationship with God through Jesus. God is the author of time and is absolutely the beginning and the end. The church needs to know that God stands at both the beginning and the end of time. That assurance is how the churches, and we, can live in hope.

Let me share a story from Parade Magazine in 2020. "Mr. Eugene Lang, a self-made millionaire was asked to speak to a sixth grade class of '59 in East Harlem. What could he say to inspire these students, most of whom would drop out of school? He wondered how he could get these predominantly black and Puerto Rican children even to look at him. Scrapping his notes, he decided to speak to them from his heart. "Stay in school," he admonished, "and I'll help pay the college tuition for every one of you." At that moment, the lives of these students changed. For the first time they had hope. Said one student, "I had something to look forward to, something waiting for me. It was a golden feeling." Nearly 90% of that class went on to finish high school."

Where does your hope come from? Where does the hope in your faith come from? Is it in prayer, worship, meditation, and study? Is it in mission work or fellowship? Is it in the preaching of the word or the celebration of sacraments? Is it in conversation with, and pastoral care provided by, your pastor? I have often

Second Sunday of Easter

been teased as being a minister of hope. I know I am optimistic, but my hope is more than optimism. My hope is in my absolute belief that God is with me, has been in the past, is in the here and now, and will be in the future. I am not alone. I am loved and embraced by the God who is and was and will be. I am redeemed by the Christ who is and was and will be. Nothing can separate me from that certainty, from that belief, for that hope.

Yes, I believe the world needs God. I believe that the world needs the Holy Spirit and the gifts it brings. I believe the world needs Jesus, while I acknowledge for my interfaith siblings Jesus is not the way they find God. When I say that my hope is in the Lord, I truly mean it, in my mind, in my body, in my soul. That is where my hope is birthed.

Where do you find hope? How do you share hope? When do you most need hope? John wrote to his churches assuring them that hope lives, as Jesus lives. This Easter season, may we know that Jesus lives. May we proclaim again and again, Christ is risen! He is risen indeed! That is where we find and keep our hope! May it be so for each and every one of us. Amen.

Third Sunday of Easter
Revelation 5:11-14

My Redeemer Lives

We continue in our Easter season to celebrate and reflect on John's vision of heaven. As we mentioned last week, John was exiled on Patmos, having a vision of the throne of God and the eschatological and apocalyptic battles yet to come. Eschatology focuses on death, judgment, and the final destiny of the soul and human beings. Apocalyptic visions are those of the complete destruction and end of the world. Much of the book of Revelation is difficult to understand and interpret, but there is wonder in this text.

Let us provide some context for this morning's reading. Imagine the vision John is having of the throne of God. The door to heaven is opened to John and he can see the magnificence of the throne of God. But there is even more to be revealed. Surrounding this throne are 24 other thrones on which are seated 24 elders, dressed as priests. Rather than quiet reverence, John experienced lightning and thunder. Everything quiverered and shook in the presence of the throne of God. John's vision continued to expand to see even more. There were four living creatures, each with six wings and covered with eyes. They mostly resembled a lion, a human, an eagle, and a human. They were continuously praising God. As they sang, the elders bowed before the throne. All bowed in honor of God simultaneously. John's vision expanded even further to include the right hand of God, which held a scroll with seven seals. Then there appeared the figure of the lamb, clearly having been slaughtered with seven eyes and seven horns. Those in the court paid the lamb homage as they had previously paid homage to God. They sang of their confidence in the lamb and the lamb's ability to open the seals of the scroll. At this point we

Third Sunday of Easter

begin our text for the day.

The heavenly court, those whom John has already seen, sang their praise to the lamb who had been slain. Yet, the chorus of their voices was joined by still more voices. Every voice in heaven and on earth sang its praise and honor to the lamb. All were centering their attention and praise on the lamb. They knew, as John and we soon would, that the lamb can and will break open the seven seals (chapter 6).

I do not know about you, but this imagery overwhelms me. The vastness of this vision, the oddity of the creatures, the ever-widening circle of those singing praise, these are beyond imagining. I am not sure where I would look first, what I would see and hear.

Have you ever seen something so beautiful that it almost hurt to look at it — the vision brought tears to your eyes? This has happened to me a few times. Of course, I have not had a vision of God enthroned in heaven, but I have seen some wonderful natural sights. Standing at the south rim of the Grand Canyon, my breath caught in my throat. Even though I hate heights and could not convince myself to hike down the trail, I looked out and down into the canyon and the most wonderful rock formations and rapids in the Colorado River. The sheer breadth and depth of the canyon was amazing to me. Tears came to my eyes as I looked at this wonder of nature.

When I was in India in 2020, I was able to see the Taj Mahal, truly a wonder of the world. The marble, the individual placement of gems and stones, the dome, all these were breathtaking. My breath caught as I walked into this ancient structure, begun in 1632 and completed in 1653, built to honor and immortalize Shah Jahan's third wife. The structure clearly is wonderful and awe-inspiring.

Yet, nothing in my human experience is at all like the spiritual experience John is describing, the experience of seeing God, Jesus, the elders, the creatures in the heavenly realm. Why this reading on this Sunday in this Easter season? Perhaps it is because it aligns well with the gospel from John.

Living in Hope

In the gospel lesson, the disciples, after seeing the risen Christ, have gone back to fishing. It is as if they have not really seen the risen Christ, as if they do not understand the magnificence of the resurrection. John's vision of heaven surely provides a counterpoint to their lack of enthusiasm or understanding of what they have seen and experienced.

We take Easter for granted as well. For many of us, Easter is just a day, surely it is a day to celebrate in worship, to receive communion, to shout the praise that Christ is risen! Yet, by Easter Monday most of us have gone back to our routines, just as the disciples do. Has the resurrection meant so little to us? Or is it that the concept is so excessively big that we cannot begin to comprehend it?

Easter is a season, my friends. Resurrection is a promise that continues to live on throughout the hours, days, years, millennia since that first Easter morning. We, the faithful, those who carry the love of God and the light of Christ within us, live into that resurrection, that hope of resurrection every single day — or, we should.

Sustaining awe and wonder is difficult. It is hard for us to know and feel the joy of the resurrection moment every single day. Awe is challenging for us to cling to. Maybe it is less important to hang on to awe, than it is to live in the hope that we have been given through the life, ministry, death, and resurrection of Jesus. Maybe the hope is enough.

Do you live in hope? Where do you find hope? The Easter season sets Christians apart from other faith communities. We truly are Easter people. It is Easter that is the foundation of our faith. The resurrection of Jesus is foundational not just to our theology, but to celebration of the life we live and look forward to. How often do you think about our resurrection faith, the hope of that resurrection guaranteed by the sacrifice, death, and resurrection of Jesus?

I do not know about you, but I do not think about resurrection every day. Surely, I know it is my hope and my future at the end of my human existence. Yet, I do not meditate on it, pray about it, think about it very often. It is like the warranty on my car. I

Third Sunday of Easter

know if something on the car stops working, I can take it in to get it fixed and the warranty or the extended warranty will cover the expense. My belief in the resurrection is a little like that. I know that Jesus lives in me. I know I put my faith in God through Christ at the center of my life. I know I try to live a life worthy of God's love, living in God's righteousness every day. I know it so well that I count on it. I do not have to think about it every moment or even every day. I can go about living my life and count on God to be with me.

Yet, occasionally, it is good to stop and reflect on the gift and the sacrifice that gave that gift. That is what the season of Lent was all about — a time to reflect on the ministry of Jesus, to focus on how Jesus lived and calls us to live, how Jesus sacrificed and calls us to sacrifice, how Jesus died, was raised, and ultimately how I too will die and be resurrected. The Easter season is the time to remember and to celebrate the resurrection.

When I visited Israel & Palestine, I traveled to many of the places mentioned in scripture. There is some disagreement about where, the exact location where Jesus was crucified and where he was entombed. The Church of the Holy Sepulcher in Jerusalem is said to be one of the possible locations for the tomb of Jesus. You can reach down through the foundation and touch the stones of the possible tomb. The other possible site is managed by the Episcopal Church and is called the Garden Tomb. Having toured both, I do not know which is more likely the site. And that is less important. As the docent at the Garden Tomb told us after we had been able to walk into the tomb and look around, "There is some disagreement as to which location is the actual tomb of Jesus, but it doesn't really matter. The tomb is empty. My redeemer lives."

Yes, friends, our redeemer lives. John's vision of heaven includes God enthroned, priestly elders, creatures, and the lamb who was slain — the Christ, Jesus. It is Jesus who opened the gates of heaven for us. It is our task to live in the hope of that redemption and to offer the gift of that redemption, through our faith, to others. Live in awe if you can, but certainly live in faith, live in hope, live in love, live in celebration of the Easter gift we have been given. Amen.

Fourth Sunday of Easter

Revelation 7:9-17

Peace In The Presence

How large is your worshiping community? When people gather for physical or online virtual worship, how many people participate? Are there 24 elders in your church? Are there 144,000 worshipers gathered at the throne of God? This is the scene John envisions in heaven.

As we have explored the book of Revelation throughout this Easter season, we have reviewed some of John's vision. We have spoken together about the throne of God, the 24 elders surrounding the throne of God, the four creatures, the heavenly host, but now, as the lamb has removed six of the seven seals on the scroll, we find 144,000 of the redeemed present at the throne. They are wearing white robes and holding palm branches.

Historically and theologically, the white robes signify purity and righteousness. The palm branches, as on Palm Sunday, indicate victory. The symbolism of heaven continues to touch John and through the writing of his vision, us. My imagination cannot really picture this scene. I try, but it seems a little beyond my reach. I have hesitated to look at illustrations or paintings reflecting this scene but I want to build the picture in my own heart and mind. The colors that come into my mind are brilliant, radiant, and varied; the auras surrounding God and the elders are gleaming, reflecting light brighter than the sun and shimmering over and around all who are gathered. The songs of the elders and the heavenly beings are melodic, filled with harmonies that touch not just my ears but my heart. It is truly beyond my imaginings.

Perhaps the point is not for me to share in John's vision or in anyone else's. Perhaps the point is to worship, where I am, how I am, in the time and place that I am. This is the important

Fourth Sunday of Easter

reminder — I am called to worship God unceasingly. Unceasingly worship when everything is going right or when everything is going badly, when I am joy-filled or when I am sad, when I am feeling brave or when I am feeling afraid. I have been called and reminded in scripture to pray without ceasing. Sometimes I am able to do that, but how do I worship without ceasing? Doesn't life get in the way of that?

At the throne of God in the heavenly temple, it seems easier somehow to worship without ceasing. God is present in that space with us, and we serve in God's presence, nurtured and strengthened by the very presence of God. Ah, perhaps that is the way I worship without ceasing. If I can feel God's presence every day, if I can believe that no matter my circumstance, God is there, then perhaps I can worship without ceasing. There have been many moments when I have felt the presence and the strengthening power of God. Have I sought God's presence in every moment? Have I readily acknowledged that I am not alone, no matter where I am and no matter the circumstances? Have you?

As I sit writing this sermon message, I am seeking God's presence. I want the words I type to come from God, to be God-inspired. I have prayed before writing, I am praying as I write. The very act of writing this message is a prayer for wisdom, for inspiration, for connection with the divine within and around me. This happens for me when I journal as well, when I put pen to paper and seek to understand my feelings, my yearnings, my hopes, and my dreams. I seek the presence of God. What I am beginning to understand is that I do not need to seek the presence of God. God is already here. What I need to do is become increasingly aware of the presence of God in all the moments of my life, in every moment of my life. The tuning into the presence of God seems the important task. It may not be as easy here on earth as it is in the heavenly temple, but God is as present here as there. I can take consolation and joy in that. I can focus on that presence as I go through my day. I am the one who turns away from God. God is always present.

Living in Hope

How do you experience the presence of God in your life? Do you experience God in family, friends, pets, nature, prayer, study, and/or work? God is in all those places with each of us. That is the miracle of God. God is in our hearts, minds, and souls every moment of every day. We just have to feel that presence. We just need to turn toward that presence and know that God is with us.

When I asked if 144,000 people were worshiping in your congregation's worship services, I was reminding us of the newest additions to John's vision. John saw 144,000 standing before the Lamb, robed in white and holding palm branches. In John's vision, one of the elders asked the seer who those white-clad individuals were. We are told that they had endured the "great ordeal." In some traditions, these were the individuals who had survived the tribulation, the period during the end times when God judged the world for its unrighteousness and prepared to establish Jesus as the king over all the world. In any case, the 144,000 have come through the ordeal and they have been cleansed and purified by the blood of the lamb, by the sacrifice of Jesus. They are martyred saints, forgiven and vindicated by God. They join the others in unceasing praise of God in the heavenly temple.

Not being an advocate for end times theology as described in the apocalyptic scriptures, I tend to view the 144,000 as the completeness of the people who are gathered to God through their belief in Jesus as Lord and their forgiveness through him. They are representative of the millions of us who are Jesus followers, a symbol of the gathering of all the faithful into the presence of God on God's throne in the heavenly temple. While not getting into a deep debate about theology, I can remember a discussion I had with a parishioner during a study on the book of Revelation. He asked me if I believed in the rapture, the bringing home of all the faithful before the end times tribulation begins. I admitted to him that I did not believe in a mass rapture experience. Rather I believed that when each one of the faithful, each follower of Jesus died and left the earth, their souls were raptured as they were brought into the presence of God. This is a discussion worth further study and I encourage you to have the conversations

Fourth Sunday of Easter

and do the studying around these concepts with theologically trained leadership. Suffice to say that in John's vision, the 144,000 represent those martyred saints of the faith, purified by their faith and belief in Jesus, gathered at the throne of God in victory. They have come home to God as we will go home to God when our time on earth has ended. They are now at peace, and more than that, they are without any need being met.

Verse 16 of this passage highlights that God excludes hunger, thirst, pain, and specifically scorching heat in the heavenly court. There is no more want, no more discomfort. The 144,000 are cared for and are free from physical constraints and pain. They can worship freely moment after moment without need and without worry. Their whole focus can be on unceasing worship. What a gift! The gift of being able to worship continually without physical need, without distraction, without any other focus on our energy and our time.

In my respite time I have occasionally visited convents, retreat centers, and monasteries. I have been amazed at a life centered on worship and prayer. There are times for work to maintain the community but there is scheduled and unscheduled time for prayer, meditation, and reflection on the presence of God. I hunger for that schedule, that order in my own life. The order for each day is kept with time for prayer, song, study, work, eating, and service to the poor. All is orderly and the stability of the practice allows the heart, mind, and spirit to focus. Somehow in my everyday life, I am less able to add this structure. In this, I sometimes admire my Muslim friends whose day is ordered by prayer five times a day. I could do so, but it seems a little unnatural to me. Perhaps that is where the practice comes in, as with the monks and sisters I know whose lives are ordered around prayer, rather than around physical needs and work. In any case, the 144,000 had nothing to focus on except worship; unceasing worship at the throne of God. What a gift and reward for the hardships they have encountered and endured.

One other key reminder is present in this portion of John's vision. The Lamb has become the shepherd. In verse 17, the

Living in Hope

lamb is seen as the shepherd who lived, guided, and cared for the sheep, the 144,000. Jesus, the shepherd, walked among the 144,000 bringing them to the spring of living water. This harkens me back to the conversation between Jesus and the Samaritan woman at the well. In their conversation, Jesus told her that he could provide living water and she would never be thirsty again. John's vision shared this concept. The 144,000 would never encounter thirst again as they had been shown and had partaken of the living water. The scriptural connections go beyond that gospel story.

This is one of the rare Sundays when it seems that all the lectionary texts connect together. Psalm 23 is our reminder that the Lord is our shepherd and brings us to springs of still water. The gospel lesson from John 10 also speaks of the shepherd whose sheep know his voice. These texts connect together and connect us in time and space to the song of the psalmist reminding us of the here and now. The gospel reminds us of Jesus' call to us and our knowledge and acceptance of his voice calling to us, as well as John's vision of the heavenly temple where Jesus, the Lamb, shepherds the 144,000. The interconnectedness of these scriptures brings me a sense of the presence of God in all times, in all places, and in all moments of life and death. We are reminded that God's presence is with us. We need only seek God and we will know God is there, here, and everywhere.

There is great peace in that assurance. There is great peace in the knowledge that I am not, we are not, ever alone. I can worship God unceasingly whenever and wherever I am, as can you. I can know the gifts of God, allaying my spiritual hunger and thirst, as can you. I can be comforted and guided by Jesus, the lamb and the shepherd, as can you. There is great peace and joy in this. Do you feel it? Amen.

Fifth Sunday of Easter

Revelation 21:1-6

Transformed And Transforming

We continue this Easter season with the epistolary readings from Revelation. In this reading, we see the final vision of the world to come: the new heaven and the new earth, the new Jerusalem. This is also an apocalyptic vision, the vision the seer shared with us of the end of the world as we know it. This is a writing about a prophetic promise of what is to come at the end of time as we know it. John's vision is almost complete and we may be comforted by this vision of what is to come.

The churches to whom John was writing and sharing his vision needed to know the comfort of what was yet to come. They were living in an oppressed society, feeling the heel of the Roman Empire on their throats, as a metaphor, and their pastor had been arrested and exiled. John's vision of the cataclysmic end of the world and the battles wrought had been disquieting and we need only read the chapters of this revelation between last week's reading of chapter 7 and this week's reading of chapter 21 to know just how cataclysmic it was. John's vision brought comfort to the people. This was what would eventually come to pass. This is how God planned to restore existence for the faithful followers of Jesus.

This portion of John's vision spoke to the creation of a new heaven and a new earth. God coming down from the heavens to establish a new Jerusalem, a new city that would shine with and through the blessings of God. This vision fulfilled the prophetic promises of Isaiah. It fulfilled the expectation that the cosmos could be changed and would be changed in an instant by the hand of God. Imagine the mountains being moved, rivers changing their course, that which was old all vanishing before everyone's eyes.

Living in Hope

This was the cosmic transformation of the world, in an instance, through the power of God. More than the transformation of the world, there was the transformation of the lives of the faithful.

God will wipe away every tear. Death, mourning, and pain will no longer exist. This is the paradise promised. Interestingly, it is not us going up to God that makes the changes. It is God coming down to earth to transform all that was and is into all that will be for all eternity. God's home is among the mortals, among us.

For me, this harkens back to the incarnation and the birth of Jesus, Emmanuel God-with-us. The people did not all accept Jesus as the Son of God, did not all follow in the footsteps of the faith in God he laid out. Jesus came to lead us into a transformation, but we were not ready or able to transform. All the rest of our lives, we might struggle for that transformation, but we were not ready in the first century to acknowledge that Jesus was Lord and that we could make the world different, align it with the will of God, be fully God's people. God had sent down from heaven a new world for us — a world without pain, loss, or sorrow; a world without hunger or thirst, a world transformed through the act of God.

Transformation is really challenging. Physical transformation is one thing. Just ask anyone who has tried to transform their health, their bodies through diet and exercise. Old habits die hard and change is difficult. I deeply admire those who have the strength and courage for physical transformation. Yet, I believe that spiritual and attitudinal transformation is even more difficult.

Just look around the world in which we live. Hunger and poverty continue to exist. Hate and violence are rampant in our world. Those with much still do not necessarily want to share with those that do not have. Racism, sexism, and homophobic attitudes still exist. We are plagued by an inability to listen to one another and strive to understand each other. We are all too human in our falling into sin and falling away from the righteous love of God and neighbor. It seems our vision is very short-sighted.

Maybe that is why this passage is a gift to us. We get to see

Fifth Sunday of Easter

the future, at least John's vision of the future, in a way that might inspire us toward transformation. At least, I hope that is what it does. The other alternative is to just live the way we always have, knowing that in the end God will fix it all. I am not at all sure that is what Jesus calls us to do or to be in our faithfulness to him.

I am of the belief that we are the light of God in the world, the hands and feet of Jesus in the world. It is our task to live as faithful followers of Jesus and that is not just about prayer and faith. It is also about action in the world. I have been and will continue to be a promoter of justice. I used to use the word *protestor*, but that word has sometimes been coopted to incite violence or anger in others. Rather I am a promoter of justice, the justice Jesus spoke about in the gospel of Matthew 25 about feeding the hungry, offering drink to the thirsty, clothing the naked, visiting the ill and the imprisoned, and welcoming the stranger. All this is the basis for my actions for justice. Are they directives or commandments? I think so. Are they our call as the faithful? I think so. Are doing these actions, participating in the care for the least among us, a way to transform that world? I believe they are.

While I am anxious for the realm of God to be in our midst, I also believe we have an individual and collective responsibility to move into the world and act for transformation in the here and now, in the moments and in the places where we live. The presence of God is shown to others when we act in these ways.

Clearly, we are reminded in this scripture, in this portion of John's vision, that God's presence is meant to be among and with the people. God lives in us. God's actions in the world are often made through us. We can be the fulfillment of the prophetic hope that love will reign, love will be shared, and that ultimately love wins. Not to be competitive, but in a world where anger and hate sometimes seem more powerful, grace and love have an important role. What happens when we love those who are our enemies, those with whom we have conflict? For me, I can see them as people in need of hope and grace and the presence of God. It is my role to share my hope, grace, and my knowledge of the presence of God with them. What if we all did so? How might the world as we know it change? Might the realm of God actually begin to live among us?

The other part of the vision is the removal of pain and hurt, suffering and mourning. God wipes every tear from our eyes. There is no more pain. That is a joyful hope. For those of us who have experienced deep loss and pain in our lives, hope is the anchor to which we hold, the dock which prevents us from drowning in our pain. Excuse the mixed metaphors, but I genuinely believe hope makes a difference.

In my late twenties, I became pregnant with twins. My husband and I were thrilled beyond imagining. I had been married before; my son was adopted by my new husband and became our son, but there was special joy in this pregnancy. My husband had been told he would never be able to father children, so we felt this miracle of my pregnancy was truly a gift from God. I was sick most of the pregnancy, new for me since I had breezed through the pregnancy for my son. As I approached the final weeks of my pregnancy, my friends at work threw a baby shower. I prepared to leave work. The following week was our wedding anniversary and life seemed to be filled with only happiness. That following Friday, the Friday before Thanksgiving, I went to the hospital for a routine ultrasound. I could tell from the face of the technician that something was wrong. She finished the scan and sent us to my doctor's office. There I was informed that both twins had died in utero. You can imagine our shock, our pain, and even our anger. God's miracle was not to be. We were sent home. I would be admitted on Sunday and would need to deliver our twins on Monday. I spent the weekend in shock, in anger, and in despair. How could this happen? I screamed my anger at God. My relationship with God was strong. I knew the relationship could stand my anger. I raged at God. I grieved with my husband and our six-year old son, who could not really understand what was going on.

Monday came. I delivered our twin sons. My parents handled the burial. My husband and I were numb with grief. And yet, I knew God was there. A friend, a Catholic priest, came to visit me.

Fifth Sunday of Easter

I was in the anguish when I asked him, "Why me?" His answer shook me, shocked me. He replied, "Bonnie, who would you wish this on? At least you have the strength of faith to know God is with you in this. It might destroy someone else's faith."

Yes, I knew God was still with me. Yes, to this day I know God is with me. We survived that loss and mourning. We survived the losses yet to come in our lives. We have held on to the presence of God, God with us in each and all these moments. My hope has been and continues to be in the presence of a loving God who lifts me up, embraces me, and comforts me in my pain. I welcome the day when there is no more pain, no more tears, and no more loss. But in the interim, in the time between now and the coming of the realm of God, I *know* God is present in my life and in all our lives. It is that hope and confidence that makes all human life acceptable and possible.

It is also why my life needs to be a part of the transformation of the world. What is your role in the world? What is your role in being faithful to our gospel mandates to love God with our whole selves and to love our neighbors? What are you called to transform in yourself, your family, your church, your community, and the world? Where are you called to act while we are waiting for the transformation of the realm of God coming down to be among us? When God does a new thing, sometimes the new thing is in us or through us. My prayer for us is that we hold on to our faith in the presence and love of God, then move into the world, acting as transformers for justice. May it be so in your time and place, in my time and place and forever more. Amen.

Sixth Sunday of Easter

Revelation 21:10, 22-22:5

The Mountain Top

I love to hike and there is nothing more amazing to me than to climb to the top of a mountain trail and look out over the vista before me; the glory of God's creation. There is a special feeling of awe that comes over me as I finish a climb and the world, it seems the whole world, lies before me.

Mountaintop experiences are prevalent in scripture as well. Moses encountering the burning bush and being called to his ministry, Moses receiving the commandments written on stone by God's own hand. Later Moses viewed the promised land he would not inhabit from the mountain top. Elijah encountered God as the still small voice on the mountaintop. The disciples encountered Jesus with Elijah and Moses on a mountain top. Mountain top experiences are profound; they change us. But in most cases, mountain top experiences are temporary. We must come down off the mountain into our regular existence.

This is not the case in these last portions of John's vision. The seer is carried away by the spirit to a high mountain. There he sees the complete vision of the new Jerusalem. In this reading we do not get the entire vision description, but the keys are there. In this city there is no temple. There is no need for a temple, for God is dwelling with the people, the very presence of God is with them in every grain of sand, every blade of grass, every drop of water. There is no need to go to a special place to worship God. God is everywhere.

During the last year as we experienced the COVID 19 pandemic and we were isolated from gathering in our sanctuaries as communities of faith, we learned some important things. We were reminded that while we love our church buildings and

Sixth Sunday of Easter

our sanctuaries, they were not required for worship. God was present with us wherever we were, wherever we gathered — in our homes, in outdoor worship spaces, in a virtual space. God was present. This learning is important to us, and it was to the people of John's day as well.

They needed to know that God was with them, everywhere, anywhere. This vision of the New Jerusalem includes us all — Jews and Gentiles, all the nations gathered in the new city of God. How wonderful to be together in the place God created for them and for us. The light of God's love and presence fills the space. Candles are not needed for certain, as the sun and the stars and the moon are not needed either. The love and light of the divine fills the space; it lights the way. The radiant love of God envelops all existence. God alone is the light. The new Jerusalem knows no night for the love and light of God permeates every space and time, every hour, and every moment.

As I have participated in worship most of my life, the light, the candlelight has meant slightly different things and been shared in different ways. We light the candles on the altar as a recognition to the light of God and Jesus. Sometimes the light leads the processional into worship. We follow the light of Christ into the worship space, onto the chancel of our churches. In some worship traditions, we light Advent candles to mark the weeks of expectation for the coming of Emmanuel, God-with-us. Each week there is more light, more candlelight, as we move closer to the light coming into the world. On Christmas we light the Christ candle, for Jesus has been born into the world. It is a candle which remains lit all during the Christmas and Epiphany seasons. Then there is the practice of taking a light from the Christ candle and walking behind it in the recessional. This signifies that we take the light of Christ into the world after worship equips us to do so.

None of that is necessary in the new Jerusalem. God's light is everywhere, infusing everything. There is no need for any other light. God and Jesus are the light in and of the world. That is a powerful image. The city knows no night. There is radiant light suffusing all that is.

Living in Hope

We are needing to be more careful in our day and age of the images of light and dark. The ancient symbol of light or white as pure and dark or black as impure has permeated our society in a new way. As racial tensions have grown, as the awareness of institutional racism has increased, it is important to be clear about our symbology. Yes, the 144,000 from last week's reading have been made pure and are robed in white, but that is not a reflection of their skin but of their robes. Black or dark-skinned people are no more impure than those of us who identify as white. We need to be cautious of our imagery and its translation into action. God lights up the world, the whole world, all the nations, as the sun, the star, and the moon have previously done. It is not a judgment on people's skin but on the source of light in the world. The radiance of God shines for us all.

The extension of the radiance of God to all the nations speaks to the open door of the heavenly realm and the new Jerusalem coming from God. The doors and gates to the city are open and will never again be shut. I often speak with churches about their openness. "We welcome everyone," they say. Yet, their actions can decry that sentiment. What they often mean is: we welcome everyone who thinks like, looks like, and acts like us. The "others" are not included or if they are, it is because they want to mold them to be just like them.

Years ago, as I taught a class on organizational inclusion, I utilized a book titled *A Peacock in the Land of Penguins* by B. J. Gallagher Hateley. In the book, the penguins were excited about welcoming a peacock into their midst. He was colorful and made a different noise than they did and was seen as creative and talented. The penguins were excited to welcome Perry the Peacock into their midst. Perry started by trying to fit in, listening and watching how the penguins did things. Soon, though, Perry the Peacock began to be more like himself, living into his peacock potential. As Perry became more himself, when he did things very differently from the penguins and the penguins interacted with them, some became annoyed. They began to ask why Perry must show off those colorful feathers. They began to ask why

Sixth Sunday of Easter

Perry did not waddle and why he made that awful honking noise. Eventually, despite their original desire to have Perry the Peacock join them, Perry left. Of course, the penguins did not understand why.

It is this kind of welcome we people sometimes offer into our faith communities? Come in, share your gifts, be yourself — *but not too much, not too fast, and not too different from us.*

This is not the new city of God as described in John's vision. All are welcomed, just as they are, from wherever they come. God's radiance is for everyone. The doors and gates are open, never to be closed again. It is a welcome we are called to emulate as we live our faith and work for transformation in our world. The limit to membership is not about the people but about their faithfulness and their presence in the lamb's book of life. That is the only requirement. It is about living in righteousness as recognized by God, not by human beings. We might choose to try and figure out who is in the book of life, but that is not our purpose. Our purpose is to know good from evil, to live into the light and radiance God provides, and to be the open doors and open gates to welcome the stranger, the lost, and the least.

God chooses. God has broken down all the barriers. There is no separation between nations and peoples. There is no separation between races and ethnicities. A new humanity, and all-inclusive humanity is a major part in this vision. All are welcome — truly all are welcome. That is the realm of God that is the New Jerusalem. That is who and what we become at the moment of the new heavens and the new earth.

In this reading from Revelation, we hear John's proclamation of the coming of a new heaven and a new earth. God has come to dwell with God's people. We are back to the promises of Genesis and Exodus — I will be your God, and you will be my people. We are back to the relationship God dreamed for us in the garden at creation; a relationship of intimacy and presence, the relationship that was severed when Adam and Eve, as identified as the first human beings, followed the temptation of evil and chose to try to be like God.

Living in Hope

Eugene Boring, a commentator I have been using in preparation for this message, said clearly that the promise of Revelation is "God does not make all new things, God makes all things new." All things — everything about our lives changes at the moment of the coming of the new heaven and the new earth. God will wipe the tears from our eyes. There will be no more death. There will be no more mourning, crying, or pain.

We are also reminded that God is the alpha and the omega, the beginning and the end — God is all there was at the beginning, and God is all there will be for us at the end… but it is enough. For John and his churches, which were under the persecution and siege of the Roman Empire, these must have been wonderful words. They must have hoped for the end of time to come quickly so they could be saved from the pain of the world in which they lived. They did not get their wish, for we are still encountering the pain and suffering, the mourning and the death of human existence. We live in the world and the world does not seem to be a new heaven or a new earth. Across the centuries, things have not seemed to have changed.

What if this is the new earth and the new heaven is with us even as we live in this time and place? Let me ask this in another way: What if the new heaven and the new earth are supposed to be lived out by us right now in our time and place?

That is a tough question, for the world does not seem like a new world. Heaven does not seem so close we can touch it. God does not seem to be dwelling with us. But what if that is our perception only and the new heaven and the new earth are here, right now?

You see, God created us to have an intimate relationship with a loving and ever-present God. God does dwell with us. God's presence is with us. Over time, we forgot that intimacy and the closeness of God so God sent Jesus, Emmanuel, God-with-us, to remind us that God is close enough to touch us, to heal us, to comfort us, to guide us, and to love us.

This morning we read about God coming to dwell with us, God making all things new, God being the beginning and the

Sixth Sunday of Easter

end. Well, is that how you see your relationship with God? Is God dwelling with you? If not, it is not because God has moved. It is because you need to invite God to dwell in you and your life. If you do not feel new, transformed through the Spirit and grace of God, why not? It is not because God is not offering to pour grace over you. Maybe it is because you are afraid of the change what will come if you ask God to take over your life, make it new, pour on the grace, and then lead your life. If you do not see God as the beginning and end of your day, as the one who hems you in, it is not because God does not want to hem you in, protect you, uphold you, for that is God's promise. Maybe it is because you are afraid to surrender and let God bind your life together.

The Revelation of John reminds us that God chose us, delights in us, finds pleasure in our life and in our relationship with God. God is ready to make all things new, right here and right now. We don't have to wait for some far off date to begin living in a new earth and feeling a new heaven and knowing that God dwells with us. We need only ask, and God will answer. We need only want to be transformed and God will provide the tools for transformation. I do not know about you, but I want God in my life, changing, pruning, renewing, rebuilding, and empowering me to be God's beloved child, to be a new creation, right now today. Don't you want that too? Amen.

Ascension of the Lord

Ephesians 1:15-23

The Balcony View

This section of Paul's letter to the church at Ephesus is a note of thanksgiving. Paul thanks the church for its faithfulness and for its passion in living out the good news of Jesus. This is an important measure of health, a faithfulness expressed. The other part of the note of thanksgiving is the recognition that the church is living out their faith, by loving, specifically, loving all the saints. *Saints* was code for other believers in those days. Saints were the people who believed and gathered in faithfulness but it also included those who could not gather whether through illness, injury, poverty, or imprisonment.

Paul celebrated the love the church demonstrated for *all* the saints. Does the church you gather with love *all* the saints? Whom do you include? Whom do you exclude?

Maybe you include those who look like, talk like, think like, and worship like you. Maybe you exclude those of a different race or color, of a different political party (yes, I know we aren't supposed to discuss partisanship in church, but we do.) Maybe you exclude blue-collar or white-collar folks. Maybe you exclude the poor who can't contribute to the financial health of the church. Maybe you exclude those who are homeless and walk into the church smelling a little or a lot, but who are hungry for inclusion and love. Maybe you exclude those who are mentally ill or challenged and may not behave in ways we understand or generally accept. How about the children who are a little rowdy and disruptive? Maybe we exclude the child on the autism spectrum. Who are you including and who are you excluding — right down to who you call to be your pastor?

As a conference minister in the United Church of Christ, I

Ascension of the Lord

speak with a lot of congregations who are seeking a new pastor. We, in the United Church of Christ, have an open call system which means that churches and pastor create profiles. Pastors choose, often based on the church profile, where they want their pastoral profiles sent. Churches review those pastoral profiles and choose who they will interview as they discern who they will call as their next pastor. Not so long ago, I was at the church governing board meeting. As I was talking about who they might be looking for to serve them while they prepared for their search, an odd and funny thing happened — especially since I am a woman, a pastor, and a conference minister. The chair of the governing board said, "We don't really want a woman."

Imagine my surprise. I, the female conference minister helping them discern their interim or supply pastoral needs, was told that only men were welcome. Coincidentally, the majority of the governing board members were women. By the end of our conversation, I had been asked twice if I wanted to serve them. I assured them I had a full-time job, but the paradox was not lost on me. We won't welcome a woman, but we will ask you both to help us and to come to us.

Who is excluded? Who is included? Which saints do we choose not to love? It's a sobering question for the church.

The church in Ephesus was being thanked for their love and welcoming for all the saints. As Paul prayed for his church, he asked God's blessing on them, praying for their wisdom and their continued revelation of Jesus as Lord and Savior. He was hopeful that Ephesus would continue to be a community of faith dedicated to spiritual understanding and that their faith would be strengthened and deepened. What a hope for a church!

In my role as a conference minister, sort of like a bishop but in a congregational polity without the ability to direct people or churches into specific decisions, I am often asked to consult with pastors and churches about their futures; about decisions not just about pastors but mission, buildings, mergers, collaborations, and a myriad other parts of church life. I do a lot of training and coaching, but I also do a lot of praying. I pray for pastors who are

Living in Hope

leading healthy congregations and not so healthy congregations. I pray for church lay leaders struggling to lead or make decisions for and with their congregations. I pray about fractures in the covenantal agreements between pastors and congregations and issues between and among congregation members. In all cases, included in my prayers, is the hope that the church will live into their call as spiritual communities, formed to assist in the birth and deepening of the faith of its members. It is a fervent prayer. It is a prayer filled with hope as I ask God to bless and nurture as well as to lead and nudge congregations into becoming the best and most faithful people they can be. I share the fervency of Paul's prayer of thanksgiving for those pastors and churches that seem to be focused on their spiritual life, their deepening understanding of God, and the mission in the world.

How are you praying for your church community today? What role are you playing in your church's health, in supporting your pastor's leadership? How are you encountering God as the church lives and moves together in worship, prayer, and mission?

This is Ascension Sunday, and it may seem odd to be focused on praying for the church as this epistle reading encourages us. Yet, we often forget the power of the Ascension. We forget that we are not just people sitting in the pew, living in the world. We are connected spiritually with Jesus in the heavenly place where he now resides. Perhaps it is important for us to view the world more broadly. Maybe we need to see the world, the universe from God's perspective rather than the perspective from our pew, our sanctuary, our car, or our home. Maybe we need the broader birds-eye view from above. In conflict situations I ask people to take the balcony view, to look at situations not from up close but with some perspective.

If we can think about our view of the world becoming a more heavenly view, we might see issues, problems, relationships differently. There was a Bette Midler song recorded in 2015 titled "From a Distance." Look up the lyrics. They are very vivd and very clear. From a distance we all have a different perspective. Paul wrote his letter to the church in Ephesus from a distance.

Ascension of the Lord

He saw a healthy and spiritual vitality in them that they might not have seen in themselves. What do you see from a distance as you look at your faith community? What is strong? What needs shoring up? Where are gifts being used? Where are gifts being squandered? How are we — how are you — living into the Ascension of Christ, the heavenly vantage point?

Paul reminded the church, and us, to live into the fullness of our faith in Jesus. Jesus' ascension reminds us of his sovereign power over all that is. As we have reflected for the past several weeks, while exploring John's vision in the book of Revelation, one of the key learnings was that Jesus reigns in the heavenly temple with God. There is no question; Jesus is Lord over everything in heaven and on earth. Focusing on the sovereignty of Jesus as the reason we gather to worship, and as the reason Paul planted churches just as forbears planted churches, expands our focus and deepens our understanding of the human and heavenly communities to which we belong.

This Ascension Sunday, let's take the long view, the balcony view. Let's take the heavenly view of who we are called to be, who we are called to welcome, who we are called to be as people of faith. Let's pray that the doors are opened wide, the strangers are welcomed, God is glorified, we are renewed and equipped, so that when people see us, they also see the light of God's love shining through us. Amen.

Seventh Sunday of Easter

Revelation 22:12-14, 16-17, 20-21

The Beginning And The End

This reading from the book of Revelation, the vision of John, reminds us that Jesus is the beginning and the end, Jesus is the first and the last, the alpha and the omega. But even more than that, this reading reminds us to come to the Christ, to come to Jesus, to come to the water of life. Jesus poured his very self out to us and invited us to be a part of the work of the faith: a disciple. We are as invited to come with Jesus on a faith journey as Peter, Andrew, James, John, and all the others who followed Jesus were invited. The question is - what will we do with this invitation? Will we come to the living water of our faith, come to Jesus, and follow him? Will we move into the shade of the tree of life and encounter the rootedness we have with all those who have believed in God? Will we see our role in the church, in the faith, as a call on every part of our lives?

In John's vision shared with us in the book of Revelation, we hear Jesus sharing his ancestry as a descendant of David, an essential relationship as the new church is formed from the Jewish people. But Jesus did not stop there. Jesus reminded John, and us, that Jesus would come once again. Jesus will come to be with his people, with the disciples of the faith those who choose to live in faith, hope, and resurrection.

On this Seventh Sunday of Easter, have we forgotten the joy of Easter morning? Have we gone back to the everydayness of our life here in this time and place? Or do we awake with a sense of hope and the presence of the living Jesus in our midst. Where is our faithfulness? If we were asked to write and share our statements of faith, what would we say? Not repetitive words of creeds, famous prayers, or hymns, but what are the deep beliefs

Seventh Sunday of Easter

of our hearts and spirits about God, Jesus, the Holy Spirit, and our role in the church as the faithful people of God? It's a question worth asking and a question worth answering.

In the good days, at the celebrations, when everything was going the way we wanted, it was easy to be joyous and hopeful in our faith. It is when times get tough, sad, or difficult that hope can be hard to find. I have an assignment for you. Sometime in the next week, take a moment in your prayer time to think about what you believe. If you were asked to share a statement of faith, the essence of how you experience God, Jesus, the Spirit, and your role in and through the Christian church, what would you share? Write this statement on paper, pray over it, encounter it in prayer, revise it, rewrite it, until it is the essence of how you experience your faith. You do not have to share it publicly, although it might be a wonderful experience to share them with each other. Read this statement as a part of your prayer ritual and let the words bring you into closer relationship with our God.

Jesus shared his belief and faith every day in his encounters with the disciples, with the strangers, with those who needed wholeness and healing, and even with those who questioned and ridiculed him. A part of Jesus' prayer for the faithful was included in John's gospel that will be shared this morning. This is a prayer offered on the night he was betrayed and arrested. Jesus prayed a prayer of intercession for us: "I ask not only on behalf of these, but also on behalf of those who will believe in me through their word, that they may all be one. As you, Father, are in me and I am in you, may they also be in us, so that the world may believe that you have sent me."

Jesus' prayer became a foundation for the forming of the United Church of Christ, that they may be one. This is the denomination to which I belong, a united and uniting church. Jesus is not seeking, nor is the United Church of Christ seeking, that we all agree with every word we each say, every word which preachers preach, or Christians say. Rather Jesus went deeper than that. Jesus asked that just as God and Jesus are one, in love, we too are called to be one. It is the love between Creator and Christ, between Christ and Spirit, between Christian and Christian that is the key. This prayer is all about being one in the love of God and in the love of one another. Do we do that? Do we love everyone at their, and our, very core?

We are called, as people of faith, as followers of Jesus to invite others into discipleship — not to believe everything we say or experience — but to know, through us, the love of God, to see the fruits of the Spirit of God: love, joy, peace, forbearance, kindness, goodness, faithfulness, gentleness, and self-control (Galatians 5:22-23). That is how people are invited into discipleship. It is not through rules and laws, although those can be important. It is not through how we interpret the holy scriptures, although that can be important. It is not through acts of charity and generosity, although those are important. Rather, people will encounter the living and risen Christ through our love. As the hymn says, "They will know we are Christians by our love."

It is our call, our commission, to make disciples of all nations. We do not do that through doctrine, scriptural interpretation, or through teaching and preaching. We make disciples of all nations by our love — and friends, the only way people know we love them is if we are willing to be in relationship with them. Our call is to go out — yes to invite people in — but to go out into the world and love, care, and build relationships with those who do not know God, who have not felt the moving of the Holy Spirit, with those who do not know Jesus. That is our call, to make disciples. As we reflect on our own faith, on our own beliefs, can we, will we, be about the work of the church — the sharing of love and the making of disciples?

Here is a truth: Jesus came to bring unity. He restored unity between God and humanity. He gave unity among people. All this he achieved when he gave his life for the life of the world. In the wretched darkness that was Good Friday, the star of unity, Jesus our Lord, shone brightly for all to see.

But, let's be honest: we still do live in a disjointed, divided, and discordant world. Until our Advent Lord returns to restore all things and bring unity into full completion, we will still have

Seventh Sunday of Easter

the remnants of disunity around us. Let me give you one stark example.

Today in Palestine, there is a wall around the little town of Bethlehem. There the thousands of people who live in that city are more or less held captive to their situation. The Bethlehem wall is a symbol of sad divisions that still exist between people.

Just like the Berlin Wall of days gone by, the Bethlehem wall has graffiti and messages painted all over it. One message reads, "This wall may take care of the present, but it has no future." Another message echoes the words of President Reagan in Berlin, "Tear down this wall." Yet another message cries out, "We all bleed the same color." Another simply reads, "Forgive!"

My friend Reverend Loren McGrail was a missionary in Palestine. From her I know that things continue to be difficult in Bethlehem. There seems to be no unity… and yet the star of unity is still shining in Bethlehem today. The star of unity shines through the Christians, Jews, and Muslims who work together for justice and, for those who stand up to the occupation of the Palestinian territories, for those who love and act on that love in every interaction they have.

Brothers and sisters, let us be crystal clear, the star of unity will shine brightly as we find our unity *not* in our skin color, ethnic background, common language, or common socio-economic status, but faith; in abiding together in faith, hope, and love.

As the noted Christian author, A.W. Tozer, once wrote, "Has it ever occurred to you that one hundred pianos all tuned to the same fork are automatically tuned to each other? They are of one accord by being tuned, not to each other, but to another standard to which each one must individually bow. So one hundred worshipers meeting together, each one looking away to Christ, are in heart nearer to each other than they could possibly be were they to become "unity" conscious and turn their eyes away from God to strive for closer fellowship. Social religion is perfected when private religion is purified." [in Tozer's book "The Pursuit of God"]

My friends, in Christ… we *are* one! I love what G.K. Chesterton

Living in Hope

once wrote, "We are all in the same boat in a stormy sea, and we owe each other a terrible loyalty." We could name our boat on the stormy sea, "Transition." We owe each other fierce loyalty. We owe Jesus our faithfulness and our allegiance. We owe God, as an offering of gratitude, a righteous life, a generous life living out the faith we have and hold until the new heaven and the new earth come to be. Together, together — we can abide in faith and hope and love. That was the prayer of Jesus, the beginning and the end, the alpha and the omega, prayed for us. May it be so. Amen.